How would you feel if you were told your firstborn son was born with a rare cancer? How would you feel if you were told, after weeks of treatment and hopeful signs, that the cancer was incurable and he was going to die? How would you feel as he died in your arms on Christmas Day? Andy and Jennifer tell us exactly how it felt. This book is searingly honest. It does not disguise the pain and the heartbreak. But it is also astonishingly full of faith and joy and hope. And through it all little Oliver still smiles and will break your heart as you read his story.

Alex J MacDonald, Minister of Buccleuch & Greyfriars Free Church, Edinburgh

Andy and Jennifer first came to St Peters when they moved to Dundee shortly after their marriage. Although they were only with us for one year, they were very much part of our fellowship and we all rejoiced with them on the arrival of baby Oliver, just after they left the city. To that shared joy was added a shared sorrow, when we heard the news of Oliver's illness. It was, and still is, a source of amazement at how well Andy and Jennifer managed during those difficult months. They are a testimony to the sustaining grace of God, and my hope is that others will be encouraged, helped and supported as they share *Love Oliver*.

David Robertson, Minister, St Peter's Free Church, Dundee

Love Oliver is a beautifully written, moving and thought-provoking testimony to authentic Christian commitment amidst the harsh realities of a broken world. I can hardly recommend it warmly enough. It is honest and clear, especially as it recounts the amazing bravery that Andy, Jennifer and of course, Oliver, exhibited. You will find it heartwarming and at times heart-rending, full of faith but without facile answers; at times extremely amusing, at others disturbing. Above all this is a book about faith holding firm when everything seems against it. Ultimately its hero is a God who can be trusted.'

Andy Bathgate, Chief Executive, Scripture Union Scotland

Words simply fail me as I try to capture the profound impact that *Love Oliver* has had on me. Every emotion has been stirred and the stains of the tears are still on my cheeks as I reflect on what God has done, and is still doing, through the painfully short, but wonderfully full life of baby Oliver Gill. Love Oliver is truly one of the most moving and faith inspiring books I've ever read. Love pervades every page, the reality and comfort of knowing God's presence, grace and peace in even the most tragic circumstances of life are affirmed and the incredible faith expressed by his Christian parents in both their words and actions throughout bring honour and glory to the Lord they both love and trust.

Kevan Leckie, Church in Community Advisor for Tearfund Scotland

Andy and Jennifer have faced their worst nightm
to cancer before he was six months old. Here th
with which they fought for Oliver's life. They als
the nightmare of losing their darling little boy.

D1146687

humour, courage and love with which they faced these battles. Above all this is a book about holding onto hope when our dreams are shattered. That makes it a great book.

Neil MacMillan, Mission Development Officer, Free Church of Scotland, Edinburgh

This is a profoundly moving and honest account of Oliver's tragically short life. A baby born with a devastating cancer, but to parents whose strength, courage and love knows no boundaries. Parents who shared with the world their heartbreak while at the same time giving Oliver his own little voice through his 'blog'. Displaying a sense of humour despite their overwhelming sadness, their belief in God's purpose remained at the core of their inner strength and led to a story which has deeply affected people around the globe.

Tricia Johnstone, Nurse, CHAS@Home

This is an inspirational story about "gorgeous boy" Oliver. It is about love and faith in the face of life threatening adversity. Prepare to be overwhelmed by the courage of Andy, Jennifer, Oliver and his wonderful family.

My colleague Dr Mark Brougham, who was Oliver's primary consultant, has described in his foreword the huge challenge we were all faced with. Despite everything you wowed us all with your smiles and your happy face. We are left with happy memories of a special wee boy who touched all our hearts.

I wanted to say thank you Oliver for training so many medical students. You were so calm and so clever, so handsome and wise. As a result of meeting you they will be better doctors in the future.

Through your blog and this wonderful book you have touched the life of so many people, I know your story will be a source of strength to others who face similar overwhelming challenges. Thank you Oliver, Andy and Jennifer for reaching out and telling your story.

Please support loveoliver as this charity works hard to fund the research that is so desperately needed into rare tumours that are so difficult to cure in children. Read this book and please support loveoliver in whatever way you can.

Professor W. Hamish Wallace, Consultant in Paediatric Oncology,
Royal Hospital for Sick Children, Edinburgh

Love Oliver

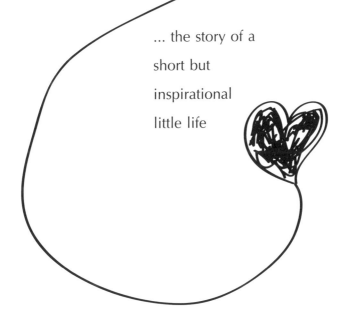

... the story of a
short but
inspirational
little life

Andy and Jennifer Gill

CHRISTIAN
FOCUS

To Our Gorgeous Boy

Oliver

'I will trust in You alone,
for Your endless mercies follow me,
Your goodness will lead me Home.'
Psalm 23

Cover image: Oliver smiling at one of his favourite things – the monkey on his bedroom wall-paper. The monkey is used as an image on the back cover of the book.

All royalties from the sale of this book are going to
LoveOliver - Registered Charity in Scotland, Number: SC042450

Copyright © Andy and Jennifer Gill 2011

ISBN 978-1-84550-807-4

10 9 8 7 6 5 4 3 2 1

Published in 2011 by
Christian Focus Publications,
Geanies House, Fearn,
Ross-shire, IV20 1TW, Scotland
www.christianfocus.com

Cover design by Daniel van Straaten
Cover Photo © David MacLeod Photography
Printed by Bell and Bain, Glasgow

Photos on page 65; 72 and 77 © copyright David MacLeod Photography

Contents

Foreword

OLIVER WILL ALWAYS be a very special little boy, and his parents, Jennifer and Andy demonstrated remarkable courage and compassion during his short, but hugely inspirational, life. Their moving story has touched the hearts of many across the globe, and it is a story that has not yet finished. With incredible strength and determination Jennifer and Andy are focussing on raising money in Oliver's memory. These funds will be used for both research and providing support to families of children with cancer, and the LoveOliver charity is going from strength to strength. Love Oliver is a fitting title for this work as throughout this book the sense of love and devotion shines through. Many may presume that a story of such a young baby with cancer must be a dark and negative tale. By contrast the overwhelming message is positive and full of hope. It is testament to Andy, Jennifer and Oliver that they can convey these feelings, and reflects the strength they derive from their faith in God.

I first met Oliver at the 'Sick Kids' in Edinburgh, when he was referred from Dundee shortly after he was born. He was an incredibly contented baby and it was easy to see why he became affectionately known as 'Gorgeous Boy'. It was not clear initially what was causing the lump in his armpit and weakness in his arm. It was hoped the mass would be benign but the biopsy result demonstrated otherwise, confirming a diagnosis of Congenital Rhabdoid Tumour. Scans at this time also showed that the tumour had spread to his liver and skin. This type of tumour is very rare, affecting about two to three children in the United Kingdom per year. They are also extremely difficult to treat as they are notoriously aggressive. However, we commenced chemotherapy with the aim of shrinking the tumour sufficiently to allow surgery to remove what remained. Chemotherapy would also target the areas in the liver and skin. Although we knew the prognosis was not good, we were fully committed to achieving a cure and ensuring the cancer never returned.

Not only did the tumour respond well to chemotherapy initially, but I was astounded by how well Oliver tolerated this treatment. Given his young age I was expecting Oliver to be very unwell, requiring being on the ward for most of the time. In particular I felt Oliver would need help with his feeding. Clearly I did not know Oliver! Not only did Oliver thrive throughout his treatment, he did not require any nutritional support. In addition to feeding well, Oliver remained a contented happy baby throughout his treatment. There were times when he must have been feeling terrible, but he still had an infectious smile on his face. His relaxed and positive personality was a clear reflection of Jennifer and Andy, who both demonstrated these attributes. Having a new baby can be difficult enough, but it is incredible how the family coped given the serious situation they faced. Support from extended family and friends certainly helped, but their faith in God was essential to give them the strength required for this arduous journey.

Given such remarkable progress during the early part of treatment it is difficult to put into words the feelings of devastation when further scans, performed to prepare for surgery, demonstrated the tumour had increased in size and had also spread to Oliver's lungs. It was difficult for me to comprehend such news as a health professional, and as such I cannot even begin to imagine Jennifer and Andy's emotions when I explained to them that Oliver could no longer be cured. Despite this devastation Jennifer and Andy remained focussed and committed to ensuring Oliver enjoyed special times with his family, and created memories that would last forever. Not only did they work tirelessly to achieve this, but also, through their faith in God, remained determined that Oliver would be cured. The ability to do this takes tremendous strength and courage, both of which Jennifer and Andy have in abundance.

Survival from childhood cancer has actually improved significantly over recent decades, with more than eighty percent of children now achieving cure. In part this is due to international collaboration to enable experts throughout the world to share ideas and drive research forward. However, despite this, some types of cancer, such as rhabdoid tumours, remain very difficult to treat. We need to develop a much greater understanding of these rare tumours in order to target treatments more effectively. Money raised by the LoveOliver charity will contribute to this research, thus directly benefitting children diagnosed with these tumours in the future.

Oliver's funeral, on New Year's Eve, was a deeply moving experience. A very special day for a very special boy. The service was truly a celebration of his short life, and his blog formed a significant part of this. His blog has charted the family's journey and is a poignant illustration of the immense challenges faced within an unfamiliar and frightening situation. It also provided an invaluable support mechanism, and I know Jennifer and Andy derived much comfort from the kindness and prayers received from people all over the world.

Although I remain desperately disappointed that I could not have done more to help Oliver, I feel incredibly privileged to have been part of this journey, and trust that you will find this story immensely thought provoking, up-lifting and, indeed, truly inspirational.

Dr Mark Brougham,
Consultant Paediatric Oncologist,
Royal Hospital for Sick Children, Edinburgh

Introduction

THIS SHOULD HAVE been one of those times in life when it's possible to say 'life does not get much better than this'. We sat on the recliner leather sofas looking out of the French windows at the beauty of creation. We agreed it was the most stunning place we had ever been to as we looked out on the hills, the beach and the bright orange sky as the sun set over the sea. Six weeks after Christmas we had taken a trip to the beautiful island of Harris. We were staying in a friend's amazing house in Luskentyre with the most spectacular views. We went for long walks on the unspoiled

beach. We ate fresh eggs from the hens and spent our evenings in front of the peat fire. We did not have anything to worry about – we were on holiday and even our meals had been provided for us.

However, we knew all too well that, for us, life could have been a lot better than this. Oliver was not in the back of the car on the journey with us. There were no nappies to change or feeds to prepare. The car was not packed full with his travel cot, toys, pram and clothes. There was no Oliver to sit and play with, cuddle on the couch or to take down to the beach to be introduced to sand castles and paddling. It was not about feeling guilty about enjoying ourselves. It was about not being able to really enjoy ourselves in the first place because the most important part of us was missing. It felt so strange, so empty and so wrong. Having to believe that somehow, this is meant to be, is very hard.

Being able to share our story with you is the last thing we wanted to do. We wish there was no story to tell. If there was no story to tell then Oliver would still be with us – we would be cherishing each precious moment with him and he would be loving every minute of life. But we are able to share our story with you, and we know that is because Oliver's life came with great purpose. Putting this book together means that we are no longer able to hold Oliver in our arms, no longer able to play with him or hear his giggles and no longer able to look forward to him complete his treatment, and to watch him grow up. Being able to write this book does mean that Oliver is safe in Heaven and that we are longing for the day when we get to meet him again there. Being able to write it means that we are able to share with you the story of our gorgeous and inspirational little boy.

It was hoped that the lump the midwife discovered in Oliver's chest when he was only four days old, and the weakness in his left arm were due to birth trauma. It could have been that the lump was some kind of cyst which would be easily removed. We never would have expected the turn our lives were about to take. It still does not feel real that the consultant knelt down in front of us as we held our two week old baby and told us his condition was actually very serious. 'A very rare and very aggressive form of cancer, a malignant rhabdoid tumour', were the words he used.

Prior to his birth, we had always said we would not be putting photos of our baby on Facebook, maybe just one or two to show him off, but otherwise we had wanted to keep our little family to ourselves. Little did we realise then that Oliver was about to have his own Facebook page with over two thousand four hundred friends! Two weeks into his treatment we decided to set up a blog for him and used Facebook and e-mail for this. It allowed us to share our prayer points for Oliver and update people about his progress without having to repeat ourselves over and over in texts and phone calls. People were able to offer words of encouragement and comment on his photos, all of which was a huge help to us. Prayer played a powerful part in our journey and the blog played a powerful part in prayer. At the end of week one on the ward we sat down with Oliver to set up the blog and write our first entry. We had not thought too much about it, but then it occurred to us that it might be nice to write updates from his point of view along with our prayer points for him. Through the blog, hundreds of people got to know our baby boy, and really felt part of his life as they shared the highs and lows of his journey with us. Within two days we were amazed to see our baby's blog had over two hundred members, and so the fact that he now has over twenty four hundred from twenty three different countries is just incredible.

What follows in this book are the entries of 'Oliver's Blog' – a blog read by hundreds on Facebook and sent out to hundreds more on e-mail each week. It takes you through the good times, the bad times and the joys and the sorrows of Oliver's short but inspirational little life. Chapter 1 covers weeks 1–12 of the blog. Following on are a few of our own reflections before weeks 13–24. Next we have included the letter we wrote to Oliver which was read out at his funeral service, as well as reflections we have now been able to make on our journey with him, and with God. Our hope is that through reading Oliver's story, his lifesong will continue to make a lasting impression and bring a smile to many. We also hope that through Oliver's lifesong, God would continue to be glorified.

Weeks 1-12

30th July - Oliver

I thought I'd give you all a quick review of my life so far before letting you know how things are now. Okay, so it all started three weeks ago on July 10th. I was due on Daddy's birthday but I was fourteen days overdue. Mummy and Daddy had been hoping I'd come earlier but are now thankful that I waited till I was a bit bigger cos it means I am bigger and stronger for what's going on now.

I had a few breathing issues to begin with – due to the excitement of meeting everyone, so we were in hospital for a few days at first. During that time the doctors noticed I had a lump on the left side of my chest. They didn't think it was anything to worry about but since then I have had four ultra sounds, two MRI scans, one CT scan, one biopsy and one x-ray. I am building up a nice collection of bravery certificates and stickers which Mum and Dad say will be good for 'show and tell' at school when I'm older.

It was cool to get out of hospital. I have a funky car seat and we have just moved to a nice new house where I have my own bedroom and a garden to play in. Daddy plans to get more grass put down so we can have goal posts for playing football.

We were home for a couple of days then had to come to the Sick Kids Hospital. That's where I had my biopsy. I was made to fast for a few hours. Needless to say, I was not very impressed but Granny Black had the genius idea of getting me a dummy to keep me going, and I enjoyed sucking away on that! We got home for a few days which was fun. I got to sleep (I honestly did sleep some of the time) in my Moses basket and we went to visit Mummy and Daddy's friends in Elie. Also all my aunties, grandparents and my uncle came to visit and I got to meet my Great-Gran and Great-Aunt too.

Then we came back to the Sick Kids' hospital for a check-up and we were told that I have a very rare and serious form of cancer which needed treatment to start as soon as possible. This was very upsetting news for everyone. Since then we've heard of so many people who are praying for me and my family in lots of different places in the world. I thought it would be a good idea to keep everyone up to date by writing this blog. My family and I really appreciate everyone's support and prayers. We know we have a long and difficult road ahead but we also know that we have an all-loving and all-powerful God in control who is looking after me. Now to let you know how my first week here has been going:

One of our first family photos

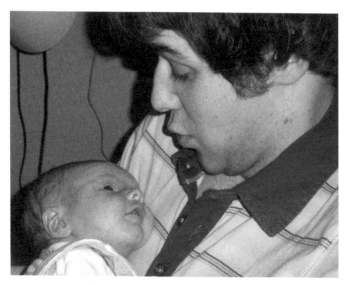

Having a father and son chat

Week One at Sick Kids

We came to hospital on Sunday night and on Monday I had an operation to get a central line put in. It's not the nicest thing to have but it does mean no more needles for blood tests or anything – hurray! I needed to have a second operation because the line had come out of place but it is fine now. It did mean I had to fast for most of the day but my dummy saved the day.

On Tuesday and Wednesday I had my first lot of chemotherapy. It went well and I haven't suffered any side effects which is good. The doctors are hoping that in twelve weeks' time the lump I have will have shrunk down enough so that they will be able to remove it. The doctors say that although it's difficult, they are treating me to cure me, and they are happy with how I'm doing so far.

On Thursday I was able to go for a walk in the park with Mummy and Daddy. Today I went with them to get my birth certificate, so

I am now legally a human being! I have had lots of visits from my grandparents and from Uncle Alasdair and Auntie Esther so that's been nice. Cousin Donald from Stornoway came too, and also Mummy's friends Kate and Catriona so I've had lots to keep me busy and keep my mind off what's happening.

The nurses all like to 'get a cuddle' from me and everyone tells me how gorgeous and chilled out I am! Apparently I'm also very alert for my age. Mummy and Daddy have been teaching me lots of songs and I might be getting to go and stay at CLIC Villa with them tomorrow so I'm looking forward to that. Today I got to make ceramic prints of my hands and feet and tomorrow we're getting the paints out!

Andy and Jennifer

We are very aware of so many people praying for Oliver and for us and have had a growing sense of peace, throughout the week, that God is in control. People have been asking how best to pray for him so here are a few things.

Thank God for:
- a good first week with Oliver responding well to treatment and staying content and happy throughout all he's having to cope with.
- the fact that feeding, sleeping etc. is all going well and normally.
- the fantastic team of doctors and nurses who are working to make Oliver better.
- that we have been given accommodation and that Oliver has been able to come out for walks with us.

Please pray:
- that Oliver will not suffer the side effects of the chemo.
- that the lump will show signs of shrinking so that after twelve weeks it can be removed.
- that we will stay strong for him and be able to have him home with us at times.

- that the doctors will be given the wisdom to know how best to treat him.

31st July – Oliver

So far today I have fed A LOT and slept A LITTLE. My Great-Granny Gill came to visit me so that was nice. I am not getting any treatment today so the plan is to do some hand and feet prints with paint and to maybe go out for a walk. Last night one of the nurses made Mummy and Daddy tea and toast so that she could cuddle me while they had it. They're threatening not to let me go home cos the cuddles are so good! I have some physio exercises to do for my arm. Sometimes we have to count to ten very quickly cos I'm not a huge fan of these exercises. Please pray that I keep well till my next chemo on Tuesday and that my blood pressure goes back to normal so that I can go out and about and maybe even get to cousin Abi's church for the first time tomorrow.

1st August – Oliver

I've had a relaxed weekend – no treatment – only had regular blood pressure and temperature checks as I get ready for my next chemo on Tuesday. My blood pressure is back to normal so that is good. I made some cool hand and footprints yesterday. I didn't like the feel of the paint at first but I got used to it and then had a bath to clean myself up. Today I had my first trip to church. The singing was so relaxing I got a good sleep, then I woke up to find Abi had gone out to where the toys were, so I cried loudly enough for Mummy to take me out too. Lots of people knew who I was and said they are praying for me. Daddy realised that breastfeeding mums get free food and drink so he has become a 'breastfeeding dad'. Mummy makes him expressos to give me (she said I have to clarify that these are not coffee, they are expressed milk from her!) He enjoys feeding me. I like expressos so much I now demand them every two hours! Mummy, Daddy and I appreciate all the nice comments people are leaving on my blog and everyone's prayers – will update you soon again xxx.

2nd August – Andy and Jennifer

We have enjoyed a relaxed weekend with Oliver. We have taken him for walks, and he has had his first trip to church. The staff on the ward are all lovely and are making us feel at home here. It's amazing how quickly this feels normal. We are very grateful for all your messages of prayer and support which are really helping us stay positive through this time.

Please pray:
- for Oliver's left arm. The movement is very limited and we are not sure if it's due to the lump pushing on his nerves. He has physio exercises to do which we hope will begin to improve mobility. It will be a while before we know how much his lump is affecting the movement.
- that his next dose of chemo goes well tomorrow and his blood pressure will go back to normal.
- that he won't pick up any infections when his blood counts drop (this tends to happen seven to ten days after chemo, so about now). They are good just now and we are thankful for this.

Give thanks:
- that he is feeding and sleeping well, as well as being quite chilled out and very alert.
- that he is responding well so far and that doctors are happy with his progress.

My first of many Gorgeous Boy smiles

4th August – Oliver

Firstly I have to say I am excited about having so many Facebook friends and look forward to meeting everyone! My week is going well. This morning the consultant said my lump is looking so much better, it's as if it's 'melting' away – softer, smaller and a much better colour. They're going to scan me in five weeks instead of twelve to see how things are. My blood cell counts are a bit low at the moment. This is normal and expected, but it does mean I'm more prone to get infections, so I have to be very careful. The consultant is amazed at how alert I am and said they don't want to ever let me home cos they've all taken a shine to me, and they fight over who gets to come to do my daily check-ups! Mummy and Daddy have other ideas about me staying here forever though! I had chemo yesterday. It was just a quick dose this time and my next is not till next Tuesday.

Yesterday I met David Robertson. I recognised his voice from when I used to go to his church before I was born! Then Auntie Esther and Abi came to see me and we went out for a walk. Today I've been chilling out with Mummy, Daddy and Granny so far. I pooed in the bath yesterday – it was quite funny! I've started smiling too which has got everyone on the ward very excited! I really like looking at lights and so I've been given one which shines on the ceiling in my room – it's pretty cool.

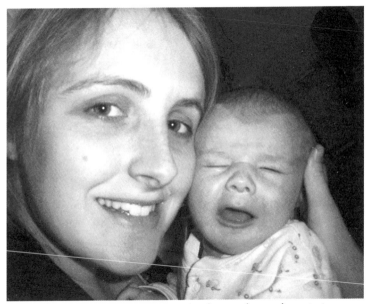

Daddy taught me to make funny faces for photos

Andy and Jennifer

We are very thankful that Oliver's lump is showing definite signs of improvement – smaller, softer and better colour. Praise God! Doctors have been very positive about his progress so far.

Prayer Points:

- Oliver's blood cell counts are a bit low at the moment. While this is normal and expected in between chemos, it does mean he is more likely to get infections, so we need to be very careful. Please pray that he is protected from them. He will be getting a daily injection in his leg to help counts go back up more quickly.
- Please pray for his physio to continue to improve the movement of his left arm.
- While we are really pleased and encouraged by his progress so far, he does still have a thirty week treatment plan. We won't be in the hospital all the time. Providing he is well enough he will be at home and come in for chemo. If he has a temperature he would need to be kept in hospital. Please pray we will stay positive and manage to take one day at a time.

6th August – Oliver

Friday nights are very quiet here so I have a chance to update my blog. I'd been hearing the word 'temperature' a lot and I wondered what it was. Having now experienced one for myself I'd ask you to please pray I don't get many more! I haven't been allowed to go outside for forty-eight hours in case I catch any infections. Hopefully I'll get out for a walk tomorrow.

We liked my visit from my consultant this morning. He said I'm doing as well as I could possibly be doing, that the change in my lump is amazing (he hadn't seen it for a few days) and that he's VERY impressed with me. Mummy and Daddy were VERY happy to hear this. He kept saying I'm a clever boy but I'm more than sure it's down to all the prayers you guys are saying for me. My blood counts are a bit low (this is normal, as is the temperature) so I've been given some extra blood today, and an injection in my leg to help my counts go back up more quickly. It hurt a little but if it means I can go out again it's worth it!

Yesterday was Mummy and Daddy's first wedding anniversary. Granny and Grandpa Black came to look after me so they could go out. That was fun. They missed me though, so I got even more cuddles than usual when they got back! Aunt Esther, Uncle Alasdair and Abi came to see me today too (not that I really know cos I slept through the visit!) Granny and Grandpa Gill come home from holiday tomorrow so I'm looking forward to seeing them again and showing them how much I've grown, how well I can focus and how big my smile is!

9th August – Andy and Jennifer

We are now at the start of week three and are very encouraged by all the positive feedback we have received from Oliver's consultants as Oliver has already told you about. They say he's a little star and is doing as well as he possibly could.

This week please give thanks for how Oliver is responding to treatment and for the very positive difference in his lump. Also give thanks for him being able to move his left arm a bit more. He is very content through all he's having to cope with, and we are very grateful for this. His blood counts are now back up and his temperature has been good for a few days now. We are also very thankful that he was able to make it to Abi's baptism yesterday.

Please pray for his next chemo tomorrow. This week he just gets one short dose. He is on antibiotics at the moment for an infection caused by his central line so pray these help him to recover quickly from this. He is expected to have a good week this week, with maybe even a couple of days at home, so please pray he keeps well in the lead up to his five days of chemo next week. Also please pray that his physio will continue to improve the movement in his left arm.

Once again, thank you so much for all your prayers, support and encouragement.

August 10th – Oliver

A lot has been happening since I last blogged and I've found a few minutes to update you. On Saturday I met quite a few of Mummy and Daddy's friends and then my Great-Grandma Black came to meet me for the first time. I was on my best behaviour and she thought I was the bee's knees! I had to get an injection in my leg while she was holding me – but I think she found it harder than I did. After all, I'm an expert with injections now.

The good news is that my counts are back up so no more injections for a while. My consultant was so happy with me that he let me go to Abi's baptism on Sunday – unfortunately, I slept through the whole thing, but I believe Mummy and Daddy when they tell me I was there!

My consultant, Mark, came back from two weeks' holiday (he was the one who told us about all this cancer stuff in the first place) and he said I'm a little star and he was very pleased to see the progress I've made.

When Mummy and Daddy arrived on Saturday morning the ward was very quiet with no nurses to be found. When they got to my room they found all the nurses were there fighting over who got to cuddle me, and gutted that Mummy and Daddy were here so early to steal me from them!

I got given a train set on Sunday. I say 'I' but I should really say 'we' as Daddy is pretty into it too. We set it up in my room and played with it together. I also got given a really cool teddy bear from my cousins Serena and Paloma when I met them yesterday. I slept through that visit too but I've heard from Mummy and Daddy that they're lots of fun so I look forward to playing with them when I'm bigger and better. I'm a month old already – it's been a busy first one!

I've had my quick chemo today. I smiled my way through it. And because I'm doing so well with my counts and temperature I'm getting to stay with Mummy and Daddy at the CLIC house tonight, and we're going to go to Toys R Us to get me a bouncy chair!

Then, all going well, we'll go home tomorrow 'till Monday. The three of us are all very excited about getting some quality family time in our new house – can't wait! Please, please, please pray for no temperatures in that time! Please also pray I sleep really well at night. (By the way, it was Mummy and Daddy who added that last sentence in!) Next week I'll be in hospital from at least Monday to Saturday, and probably longer, because they're keen to keep me in when I'm most likely to get high temperatures and low counts. I'm probably going to be here quite a lot during the thirty weeks just because I'm so little, and because my condition is so rare they want to be extra careful with me. That's pretty much it for now but I'll update you soon again! Lots of love Oliver xxx.

Cuddles with Mummy in my own garden

August 13th – Oliver

Hey everyone! Just a quick update as I have lots to do! The good news is – I'm HOME!! Only 'till Monday but it's so exciting and

I'm loving every minute. I hope I will be well enough to have more times at home during treatment. On Tuesday I went with Mummy and Daddy to Toys R Us and chose a bouncy chair for myself. Then we had a sleepover at the CLIC house before coming home on Wednesday. I've been so good – sleeping very well during the night and entertaining very well during the day! The nurse came today to change the dressing on my central line and that went fine. My clothes are out on the washing line just now. They look so small compared to Mummy and Daddy's! Checking my temperature is always a nerve wracking moment but so far so good. If I did happen to have a high one I'd need to go straight back to hospital so please pray I don't get one. We're really enjoying relaxing and having time together at home. Will put photos up later to show you what I've been up to. Now back to all my toys ... more soon ... xxx.

August 15th – Andy and Jennifer

We have been able to enjoy a few days at home as a family.

- Give thanks that Oliver was well enough to be allowed home, and for the quality time we have had together away from hospital.
- Please pray that Oliver will be well enough for more home times and ultimately for him coming home for good. Oliver has five days of chemo this week which is the most yet.
- Please pray for his little body to cope well with this and not to suffer the side effects. He is in till at least Saturday. He also gets the stitches out of his line tomorrow as it has now settled. Please pray for no further problems with that.
- Andy starts his new teaching job tomorrow. Please pray for him as he settles into it and is unable to be with Jennifer and Oliver as often as he'd like.
- Jen's mum will be staying with her at CLIC during the week, with Andy visiting when possible and staying at weekends

- Please pray for us all to adapt to this new routine and that we will be given the energy and strength we need.

Helping Daddy with a Kakuro he was stuck on

August 17th – Oliver

Being at home was so much fun I don't know where to start with my update! I slept really well during the nights so I'd have lots of energy for during the day. I played lots in my jungle gym and on my new bouncy chair and explored my garden and all the rooms in my house. My one is shaping up nicely but I sleep in Mummy and Daddy's room just now till I'm bigger. We went to Beveridge Park for a picnic and I saw the ducks. We also went to Asda but I did not like that. Daddy has told me all about not liking shops and so far I agree. It was really nice just chilling out at home. Now I'm back in Edinburgh and it's Tuesday already so I thought it was time I gave you guys a wee update ...

I'm so happy I got max time at home with no temperature. I came back to the ward on Monday. I got the stitches taken out of my line now that it's settled! I'm pleased to say it didn't hurt – in fact, I smiled during it! I then started my big lot of chemo and fluids which means I'm connected to a drip for most of the week but I can still be cuddled so it doesn't bother me much.

Daddy had to start his new job yesterday but he came to visit Mummy and me in the evening. I was so excited cos I didn't expect to see him till Wednesday. He gives great hugs and sings funny songs to me in funny voices!

I totally surprised the consultants and physiotherapist this morning with how much I can move my left arm. Everyone who sees it is amazed at the progress. Chemo has made me feel a little bit sick but visits from all my grandparents, Auntie Jo and Kate have helped.

Mummy and I got a lesson in baby massage today. It was very relaxing. I especially enjoy my feet being done! More soon ...

August 19th – Oliver

I have a couple of pretty cool things to tell you. Firstly, I get on really well with my consultants and yesterday and today I've been helping them train students! One of them guessed that I was four months old. I took this as a compliment. (I'll be six weeks on Saturday).

I reckon I could be a consultant when I'm older. I've seen all four consultants the last couple of days and they're all very impressed with the positive difference in my lump, the increased movement in my arm and how calm I am about everything. They say there's still a long way to go but that I'm doing really, really well and they're very pleased – I'm the star of the ward! So after training the students I settled down for some baby massage with Mummy. I especially like my legs and feet being done. I spread my toes out to make sure they all get a shot. Daddy and Grandpa Black came to visit last night so it was great to see them and today I got visits from my Grandpa

Gill, Fun Aunt Cath, Honorary Auntie Kate and Great-Aunt Maggie – good to see them all.

Now for the best part – I get my last lot of chemo for this week tomorrow, then no more for two weeks. And guess what happens for those two weeks (providing my counts aren't too low and my temperature is not too high) ... I get to be at home!

YEY! Daddy will come after work tomorrow (can't wait to see him!) Then we will go home on Saturday morning. I may need a little blood transfusion before heading off but it's just going to be so good to go home. I'll need to be careful to keep clear of anything that could give me an infection so please pray that I'll stay well and be able to have a fun and relaxing time away from here.

Will keep you updated ...

August 21st – Oliver

This is just a really quick update to let you know that I've made it home! I got a little blood transfusion this morning and then came home with Mummy and Daddy. It was so good to be out and about again that I stayed awake the whole journey home!

We then went to the Scripture Union Big Celebration at Lendrick Muir (where Mummy and Daddy met!) I got to meet lots of nice people there who said they were praying lots for me. Now I'm home to all my toys and about to play a game with Mummy and Daddy, of who can sleep the longest! I'm home till at least Tuesday then I have a check-up. My counts are expected to be low so I'll probably have to stay at CLIC for a few days then maybe a few days home again before the next treatment starts (same five day treatment as I've just had).

I'll let you know how I get on ... xxx.

August 23rd – Andy and Jennifer

Oliver has now finished week four of treatment and has two weeks without any treatment. This is the time when he is most likely to get temperatures and infections due to low blood counts, so please pray for protection against these. He may need to stay at CLIC for a few days this week if his counts are low, as they would prefer him to be nearer the hospital. We will find out at his check-up tomorrow. He will hopefully have a few days home next week before the next lot of chemo. We cannot believe that is four weeks gone already. We are so pleased with, and encouraged by the way he is responding to treatment and more than ever are aware of our amazing God who has Oliver safe in His arms.

After twelve weeks Oliver will have another MRI scan and the hope is that the lump will be small enough to be removed with surgery. This is expected to be a difficult decision due to where the lump is positioned, and the risk of possible damage to the nerves in his arm. There is a very small chance that the lump will all be gone by then so please start praying for this. Either way Oliver still has to have thirty weeks of treatment but this is a very important stage which is already being discussed. Thank you for your continued support and prayers. We are very thankful to be having more time at home and for how well Oliver is coping. He was wide awake all day after having an anti-sickness medicine meant to make him tired. The consultant said, 'Yes, but this is Oliver ... he does things his own way' – and indeed he does!

August 24th – Oliver

Well guys, as expected I'm staying at CLIC till at least Thursday. My counts are a wee bit low so they'd like me to be near the ward because I'm so little. It's nicer at CLIC with Mummy and Granny than on the ward though. If I'd lived nearer they would have allowed me to go home. Mummy and my consultant are working on moving the ward to our town. Our garage is big enough and we don't use it!

The consultant said to bring my bag of stuff 'just in case'. He clearly does not realise how much stuff this boy needs. I brought a car load 'just in case'. I couldn't decide what outfits and toys so brought them all! I couldn't squeeze my gym in but Daddy will bring it tomorrow. I had to get an injection in my leg to help my counts go back up quicker. I slept through it – maybe it was a dream – I'll need to check with Mummy.

Please pray my counts go back up quickly cos if they do I could potentially get all next week at home before my next treatment ... now to tell you about my time at home.

Home was great! So much to do and so little time. There was the trip to Lendrick Muir, a trip to Kirkcaldy Free Church, visits from cousin Donald from Stornoway, Bruce and Kirsty, Grandparents,

Superbaby!

Super Smile!

Auntie Joanna and Honorary Auntie Kate, my jungle gym, lots of feeding and nappy changes, lots of cuddles with Mummy and Daddy, trying to sort my bedroom out ... I was very busy!

Remember I told you about the sleeping game we were playing ... bet you don't think I won ... well I did! I slept for seven hours which is apparently quite impressive for someone my age, but it really wasn't that hard due to my strong sleeping genes! I'm hoping for more time at home next week and maybe even towards the end of this week, but for now I'm just chilling out in Edinburgh!

August 27th – Oliver

My consultants love me so much that they want me in Edinburgh over the weekend ... that and because my counts are very low just now! This is all expected and they still say I'm doing as well as I possibly can be doing so that's really good news.

I get an ultrasound on Tuesday which will give us more detailed info about how well I'm doing and confirm that I am in fact Superbaby! I get a daily injection in my leg just now to help my counts go back up and it doesn't really bother me. Yesterday I was more upset about having to take my leg out of my trousers to get the injection than the actual injection itself! I also got a platelets transfusion this morning and am now back at CLIC. They're still hoping to get me home for a few days before my next lot of chemo but it'll probably be Monday or Tuesday now. Daddy is coming tonight for the whole weekend – YEY!! As much as I love Mummy and Granny, every boy needs their father and son time! Silly songs are on their way!!

August 30th – Oliver

Daddy, Mummy and I had breakfast in the Meadows yesterday then when we got back to CLIC I started to 'spike' (hospital lingo) a temperature. I was wearing my hedgehog jumper at the time so I thought this was quite amusing!

Anyway, although it's not been too bad a temperature they've kept me on the ward because they love me so much, and because I'm so little they want to be careful. I'm not sure what will class as not little...I've started feeding three hourly and have upped my amount in my attempt to be big enough to be allowed home more often. I now weigh 10lbs.

Anyway, we've still managed to have fun on the ward and I had a visit from my Great-Aunt Maggie and Great-Granny Gill today so that was nice. I also had a bit of a nappy explosion on Mummy's knee today and learned the word 'oopsy'. I like that word – it made me smile! My consultant said today that I WILL get home for a few days this week, so we're holding him to that. Will let you know if/when it happens ...

I was wearing my Spike the Hedgehog top when I 'spiked' my temperature – he he!

Andy and Jennifer

Oliver's consultants continue to be very impressed with his progress and we are very thankful for this. The one on duty this weekend was away when Oliver was first admitted and so did not see the lump then – having now looked at the photographs taken of it he said the difference is 'remarkable'. He also commented on what a special and calm baby Oliver is. At Tuesday's ultrasound they will see exactly how much the lump has shrunk, and they don't think the smaller lump in his groin will even show up at all, as they can no longer see or feel it. He has been on the ward again this weekend due to a high temperature, but it is back down now and hasn't bothered him at all. Please pray for him this week – that his temperature will stay down, that his counts will continue to go back up so there will be no delay in starting week seven's treatment, that we will have him home for a few days, and that Andy will be entitled to his paternity leave. Thank you all again for your continued prayers and encouragement for Oliver and for us.

September 2nd – Oliver

Firstly I'll tell you about my ultrasound then about two funny things that have happened. I quite enjoyed my ultrasound this time. The doctor talked me through what was happening which was helpful for me and kept me more calm, and I also managed to fill two nappies during it! The small lump I HAD in my groin has now gone – thank you God! And the big one has reduced significantly. My consultants said they are more than happy with how I'm doing and that it's as good as it could possibly be at this stage. The next big thing is the MRI and potential surgery so please pray for me in the lead up to that.

I'm now home for a few days which is great, and then I have another big lot of chemo next week so will likely follow the same hospital – home – hospital – home – hospital pattern as the last three weeks. Mummy and Daddy are just loving all the packing and unpacking! So, on Monday I was quite sleepy and then after my blood transfusion in the evening PING I was WIDE awake! I was having lots of fun but I'm guessing by their expressions that Mummy and Granny Black didn't feel the same at one in the morning!

The other funny thing was when Mummy was feeding me in the sitting room at 5 am a huge spider crawled along the floor but she couldn't do anything about it. If you know my Mummy you'll know what a scary situation that was for her!! One of the nurses said we need to have another baby one day so that Mummy can have a wee clone too, cos I'm Daddy's mini me! The good thing about that is that what has happened to me is really rare – not genetic or hereditary. We'll never know what caused it or when it started. My consultants say I'm unique and very special. Daddy and Mummy agree!

September 5th – Oliver

Home's been great ... good quality time with Mummy and Daddy and visits from my grandparents. This afternoon we are going to my cousin Abi's for coffee, cake and a family birthday that I'm not meant to mention! She (first clue) also officially retired this week (second clue) and she is one of my favourite people. We all got her a camera for her birthday to take lots of photos of Abi and me. We will spend the night at CLIC then I'll be in hospital till Saturday for five days of chemo. It will be the same course as last time so we know roughly what to expect.

The very exciting news is that Daddy has two weeks' paternity leave so he gets to do all my feeds and nappy changes! My MRI scan is going to be on October 12th. Mummy and Daddy are worried cos, seeing as I'm older now, I have to fast before it for four hours! If fasting is what I think it is I can see why they are worried!! Dummies don't fool me anymore and I don't like to be kept waiting! Anyway, I need to go pack my bags and fill up the car for my week in Edinburgh ...

Andy and Jennifer

We are very thankful for how Oliver is coping, for all the positive feedback from consultants, good ultrasound results, more time at home with Oliver, two weeks' paternity leave and for all our amazing family and friends. Please pray that Oliver continues to respond well to treatment without having to suffer from the side effects. He continues to be noted as a very calm and happy baby who is surprising everyone with how well he is doing, and we continue to be amazed by how many people all over the world are praying for him and sending messages of love and encouragement.

Please pray for Oliver's treatment in the next few weeks, for his MRI scan and the decisions the consultants will have to make about surgery. They will be discussing the MRI results with other consultants in the U.K. to decide what is best to do next.

> '*Now all glory to God, who is able , through his mighty power at work within us, to accomplish infinitely more than we might ask or think*' *(Eph. 3:20).*

September 9th – Oliver

My week on the ward is going well. I'm getting more and more excited as Saturday home time gets nearer. This is week seven coming to an end. I shouldn't have to stay on the ward for this many days at a time again till week sixteen – YEY! None of my treatment is bothering me and I'm still a milk guzzling machine! I spent some time this week training students. They have a lot to learn but I was happy to be able to help them! It has been noted that I'm a very awake baby – there's just so much going on I don't have time to sleep! Auntie Jo came to visit me. She goes to London tomorrow to study for a year. I will miss her but I'm nagging Daddy to find his webcam so we can still see each other. Abi visited. I let her play in my jungle and she did a cool rolling over trick. I can't wait to be able to do that. I now turn my head during tummy time so I'm getting there! Auntie Esther brought us chocolate cake. Mummy and Daddy didn't let me have any but they enjoyed it.

Granny and Grandpa Black came yesterday and noticed I'd grown even since they saw me on Sunday. Tomorrow I can show Granny and Grandpa Gill how much I've grown too. My friendship with Mr Monkey in my jungle is growing stronger by the day and I now quite like Mr Bug too.

I had a wee rash on my face earlier this week (it's all gone now). Mummy put a glove on my right hand to stop me scratching. She totally underestimated how much I can do with my left arm now. I used my right hand to help my left one scratch my face! The physio is really pleased with my left arm as the movement continues to come back. I have all my shoulder movement back, a lot of elbow movement, and my wrist and fingers are getting there too, so it's all good. Your prayers are really helping me so thank you all very much. It would be nice to have a steady temperature and high counts over the next fortnight to get maximum time at home, so please pray for that (and for me fasting for my MRI cos that may be one of my biggest challenges yet!)

September 13th – Oliver

It was great to get out of hospital on Saturday. When we got home we put a wash on straight away so I wouldn't have to go too long without having my dungarees to wear! Then Mummy and Daddy's friends Gayle and Ewan came. I think I'll have them as my friends too – they seem like good fun. Being home is so good that I try not to miss much, so I feed two to three hourly during the night, and don't sleep much at all during the day. Yesterday was fun – we went to Perth to surprise Granny and Grandpa Gill. It was my first trip to Perth. We went to the church Daddy grew up in, and where Mummy and Daddy got married, so that was special. I behaved very well and enjoyed looking at all the lights and meeting lots of new people. We then went to Granny and Grandpa's house so that was good too. Today we are having a pyjama day. It's a great way to spend a day. We're also ordering stuff for my bedroom. It's going to look SO cool. Will put photos up to show you when it's all done. Now to let you know where I am with my treatment.

We are now on week eight and I'm still impressing everyone with how well I'm coping with everything. Last week I had chemo for five days so that was a lot, but it hasn't made me feel sick. I enjoyed Daddy being on paternity leave and having all my visitors (even a big bear!) Some nurses came back after being away for two weeks and were amazed at how much I've grown. I don't have treatment this week or next. This week my counts are likely to be low so we'll go for a check-up tomorrow. We will probably stay at CLIC for a few days. I may have to get the daily injection in my leg to help my counts go back up more quickly, but so long as they roll up my trousers instead of taking my leg out of them then I'll cope. That's the worst part – the injection doesn't bother me. I won't get my normal immunizations till next summer but they'll be a doddle – I'm a pro now! Daddy has this week off work too – YEY! Hopefully I'll be at home for most of next week. Our mission is to get a whole week in our new house!

September 17th – Oliver

We've been staying at CLIC since Tuesday and will likely stay over the weekend. I've had the daily leg injection and have been very brave about it – there are worse things in life – like getting your temperature checked, wearing gloves or having to wait more than ten seconds for a feed when you decide you're hungry! I forgot to tell you when I reached two months old, so I'll tell you now that I'm two months and one week old, and weigh 11bs 7oz. My docs and nurses are very impressed with my feeding and weight. We've been out for lots of walks and last night we went to Fort Kinnaird to order furniture for my bedroom. It's just as well we had decided together what we were getting from the catalogue before we went, cos I fell asleep in the car and all through the shopping trip! Honorary Auntie Kate came yesterday. Her birthday present from me included a set of Jungle Snap Cards for her to play with me when I'm bigger – couldn't resist getting them! Got to go just now but more soon. P.S. Abi, I hope your cold gets better soon so you can come round to play.

Andy and Jennifer

Oliver is continuing to impress everyone with how well he's coping with treatment, his feeding and his development. Paternity leave has been great and has allowed us to have some quality time together at home and in Edinburgh – and it's only two more weeks till the October holidays! The physio is very happy with Oliver's left arm as its movement continues to improve, even now in his fingers. Please pray that this will continue and that his wrist will strengthen more too.

We have been in Edinburgh with him this week while his counts are low, but will hopefully have most of next week at home before more treatment starts. He has a check-up later today – his counts will be checked again and then we'll know more. He had a blood transfusion on Wednesday and has been keeping very well. The nurses always comment on the tiny amounts of blood he gets – the smallest amounts they have to give!

We are now at the end of week eight so please pray that treatment would continue to go well. Please pray for his MRI/potential surgery as it gets nearer – for the best possible results and for the decisions that will have to be made.

His consultants are 'more than happy' with him so far and one said that he is 'cruising through'. Oliver is such a happy baby, and we're having so much fun with him, and trusting God as He takes us through this unexpected journey. He is teaching us so much and helping us to deal with things in ways we never thought we would.

> '*Don't worry about ANYTHING; instead, pray about EVERYTHING. Tell God what you need, and thank Him for all He has done. Then you will experience God's peace, which exceeds anything we can understand. His peace will guard your hearts and minds as you live in Christ Jesus*' (Phil. 4:6–7).

September 21st – Oliver

Stage one of Mission 'Stay Home for a Whole Week' accomplished. We're HOME! Hurray! Mission stage two to pray for is to stay at home! I need to be well with no temperatures. O.K. so when I talk about counts needing to be high for me to get home I mean they need to be above 1 – below 1 is low and below 0.5 is really, really low. On Friday I was 0.09 but by Monday I was up to 6.34. How cool is that!? And I slept through my injection yesterday! Thanks for all your prayers for that one! We have till at least next Monday at home, then I should only have to be in Edinburgh for two days next week. After that I should get home again straight away for a few more days.

Great-Aunt Maggie gave Mummy, Granny Black and me a lift home yesterday. Amazingly she managed to fit all our stuff in her car – even my pram and all my toys which Mummy was threatening to leave behind to pick up later.

It's so good to be home. Daddy left on Sunday night to start work again yesterday and I know it was only a day but I was missing him lots. The only problem is that now he's working I need to try to be quiet when I wake up during the night. It is SO hard to be quiet when you decide you're hungry.

Mummy and Granny Black are talking about taking me shopping tomorrow. I think I might just need a feed or a nappy change every time they try to leave! Shops are not for boys! I'll let you know how I get on! I'll see if I can find anything more for my bedroom. My furniture is due to arrive today so this evening Daddy and I can get to work setting it all up! Oh yeah, and good news – breastfed babies don't have to fast for quite as long so I might just manage to fast for my MRI!

Singing 'Our God is a Great Big God' with Daddy

September 24th – Oliver

I'm trying to do my blog while keeping watch out the window for Daddy getting home. I love it when he comes home but more today cos it's the weekend! As well as all the fun we can have it also means we get to see each other during the night when I'm up!

I've had a busy few days. We went to visit the people Mummy works with and today Gwen came. It was good to see her again. I was only five days old last time we met. Then I got to meet Susan who I've heard lots about and then Deborah. I slept through her last visit so it was good to put a face to a name!

I'll be in hospital Monday to Wednesday next week for chemo, then all going well I get straight home for a few days and Daddy will be on holiday from Friday for two weeks. We've jazzed up my arm exercises with songs like 'Our God is a Great Big God' and 'My God is so Big'. It's much more fun now. Please pray I get home straight away, that I continue to feed well and that I don't have side effects.

Right, going to focus more on the window now cos he'll be home any minute ...

September 26th – Andy and Jennifer

Just a quick update as Oliver has already got you up to date with most of the news. We are now beginning week ten of treatment, so at the end of this week we'll be a third of the way through. There's still a long way to go but we've also completed a significant part of the journey and it is going quickly.

Oliver will be getting chemo Monday, Tuesday and Wednesday this week then will be home for a few days, so please pray that he copes well, continues to feed so well, makes more progress with his left arm, and that the treatment will continue to shrink the lump as we get closer to the MRI and possible surgery.

We've had a great week and look forward to more time at home over the coming weeks, especially during the school holidays, which start on Friday for two weeks. Oliver should be staying with us most of the time, whether it's at home or CLIC, so please keep praying for good temperatures and high counts. We continue to value and appreciate all your prayers and messages of support for Oliver, so thank you very much.

September 29th – Oliver

SURPRISE! I'm home already! I got home yesterday – a whole day sooner than we thought. How cool is that!? Monday's chemo was one that can make you feel sick, and it did make me feel a bit sick, but then I heard the doctors saying I would have to stay an extra night if I was still feeling sick, which was enough to make me better!

I'm home till Monday then probably at CLIC for a few days then home again. Good news this time includes being 12lbs 5oz and having more elbow control in my left arm. Everyone's amazed at how big I'm getting!

We got caught in rush hour traffic on the way home so I had to squeeze Granny Black's finger pretty tight to stop me thinking about milk. Then I slept for five hours, four hours and one hour during the night so Mummy and Daddy were quite pleased with that, and we're all nice and awake today to have lots of fun at home.

It's raining a lot so we'll play inside today, but I have so many things to do I don't know where to start! AND the rest of my furniture arrives today so it's all go!

October 1st – Oliver

I've been trying to stay awake as much as possible while at home to make sure I don't miss too much but I feel so bad because it all caught up on me, and I fell asleep when I was meant to be helping Daddy make up my wardrobe! He's done a good job without me though and my room is almost finished. I'm desperate to sleep in it but Mummy and Daddy want me in their room for now and to be honest, if it means getting fed quicker during the night, then I'm okay with it!

I've developed a new trick which involves spitting out my medicines! I do fine without them so I don't see why I have to take them. Mummy and Daddy aren't too impressed with this, especially as one of them involves halving an already tiny tablet, dissolving it in ten millilitres of cooled boiled water then taking out one millilitre to give me! Tiny doses!

Anyway, break over, time to get back to the finishing touches to my bedroom ...

Mummy and I made up a new bouncy game which I love!

Andy and Jennifer

Ten weeks down and a third of the way through! We have lots to be thankful for, such as Oliver, parents/grandparents, family, friends, prayers, doctors, nurses, CLIC Sargent, home, hugs, smiles, fun times, modern technology, medicine, walks in the park, the kindness of strangers, positive feedback, central lines, chemotherapy, physio, Oliver feeding so well day and night, the amazing team at Sick Kids, quality time together, holidays and so much more ... but most of all the strength and sense of peace that only God can give to get us through. Next week Oliver is just a day patient on Monday for a very quick dose of chemo. His counts will likely be down following on from last week, so we'll probably stay at CLIC for a few days and then hopefully home again while Andy is still on holiday. All is continuing to go as well as possible and we continue to greatly appreciate all your thoughts and prayers.

Oliver

One more thing I've been meaning to say ... when I was smaller I used to always keep my knees up like a frog does, and recently I heard a song called F.R.O.G which means Fully Rely On God. I like it and it goes like this:

> 'Our God is so powerful, nothing's too hard for Him and ... Our God is reliable, so good He never changes. God, He made me, He knows what I need, better than anyone. God, He loves me, He only wants good things for me ... so I'm gonna Fully Rely On God, I'm gonna trust Him with all I've got, I know He will never let me down ... Fully Rely on God, I'm gonna trust Him with all I've got ... Fully Rely On God ... cos He can do ANYTHING'[1] :O)

October 4th – Oliver

I'll give you three guesses about where I am. Hospital? Nope. CLIC? Nope. Home? YEP!! Totally didn't expect to be! It's great but also slightly embarrassing. We're trying to make a good impression in our new neighbourhood but everyone's going to think we're mad now ... packing the car full this morning, putting our bin out a whole day early, leaving as if we're away for weeks then coming back a few hours later! I'm meant to be watching golf with Daddy just now, but while he may be right about shopping, Mummy is right about golf!

I was no sooner on the ward today – hadn't even taken off my jacket – when I was asked if I'd help train some more students. So I did. Then I impressed the physio with the improvement in my arm and then had a good chat with my consultants. I have to go back

---

[1] From the album God's Love Is Unstoppable (Damian Herbert) © 2007 Song Solutions Daybreak.

on Wednesday and we have to go prepared to stay again, but for now we are just gonna enjoy our bonus time at home! I tried taking photos of my room for you this morning but it was too sunny so I'll try again tonight or tomorrow.

October 9th – Oliver

I've been staying at my Great-Auntie Maggie's flat in Edinburgh since Wednesday instead of at CLIC. As long as I'm in Edinburgh my consultants are happy, so we thought we'd have a wee change. They say I have to stay because my counts are low but I think it's secretly because I'm on call, in case they need me to train any more students.

Murrayfield is at the front of the flat and Daddy says we'll be going there as soon as I'm big enough. The plan is to have a chilled weekend then hopefully we'll head home on Tuesday after the MRI scan. Granny and Grandpa Gill have come to stay and I'm hoping to see my Great-Granny Gill too. I'll do my best to fast for the scan but when I get hungry, I get hungry! I'm enjoying my Daddy being on holiday and hopefully we'll get lots of time at home next week. We've found some nice walks to go on near our house and I'm just loving my new bedroom. I'm three months old tomorrow!

Andy and Jennifer

We are now about to start week twelve. We can hardly believe it's this time already, and are thankful that it is all passing quickly! This is a very significant week for Oliver as on Tuesday afternoon he has his MRI scan. This will help his consultants decide how best to treat the rest of the tumour. They know it is still there – they just don't know how big it is and what position it is in. They don't think chemo alone will take it all away, and they want to get rid of it so it never comes back. Surgery is the best option. This does involve

*I love my own bedroom in my own house
- there's so much to see and do!*

risks, particularly for the nerves in his left arm. Please all pray that the scan will go well and for the best possible outcome for Oliver.

Please pray for wisdom for the consultants and surgeons who will be making decisions about the next steps, and that what is left of the tumour will be small enough and in the best possible position to be removed, with minimal damage to anything else. Oliver has amazed everyone with how well he is tolerating the chemo, how much his tumour has responded to treatment, and how much improvement he has already made with his arm. Please pray for the best possible outcome from the scan and thank God for all those involved in so carefully treating Oliver. We won't have feedback straight away but we will let you know when we do. Thank you so much for all your prayers – they're all definitely helping and making a difference and are all very much appreciated.

12th October – Oliver

I thought I'd give you a quick update before going to bed (well, Daddy and Mummy think it's bed time, but I'm feeling wide awake!) So I really should have been wearing my Superbaby outfit today. I'm still feeding two hourly and when I decide I'm hungry I do NOT like to be kept waiting. I'd NEVER normally do this, but today I fasted from 10.30 am till 4.00 pm without complaining. I was meant to get the scan at 1.30 pm but didn't get taken till 3 pm!! I know – crazy to expect anyone to wait that long – but Mr Monkey, my dummy and Mummy and Daddy singing me to sleep kept me going and I made no fuss. I've had some big feeds since then, and although it took me a wee while to get over it, I'm now back to my happy, smiley little self. I'd no sooner finished my first post-scan feed than I was training junior doctors. Yep, that's right, not just students anymore! We've had a fun couple of days staying with Honorary Auntie Catriona and now we're HOME for a few days! Will let you know when we have scan feedback ... x

15th October – Andy and Jennifer

Our meeting with Oliver's consultant today left us with mixed feelings. We'd hoped the tumour could be removed but for now it's not possible. Its closeness to nerves and blood vessels makes it too complicated. This is not to say that it won't be possible at a later stage. Scan images are being sent to other U.K. consultants to see what they think. Another option being considered is radiotherapy. It has its own side effects so please pray it won't be necessary. It also would not be an easy decision and they might wait till the chemo is all finished. The likelihood is that a difficult decision will need to be made at some stage, with possible long term damage to his left arm. Obviously removing the tumour is most important. Good news is the cancer is nowhere else, chemo is working and Oliver is responding better than expected. He's a very happy baby who is developing normally and thriving, despite the strong treatment he is receiving. Please continue to pray for his progress and for decisions along the way.

We still don't understand why all this is happening, but we do know and trust that God is in control, and we firmly believe in the power of prayer. We're now onto week thirteen of treatment which will involve one night on the ward. We hope to be home again on Tuesday. We have very much enjoyed Andy being on holiday and please remember him as he returns to work on Monday. All of this is definitely not stopping us from enjoying every minute with Oliver. The words of this song keep coming to mind so we'll finish this post with them:

> '*Sometimes my prayers seem so empty, Your voice seems so far away, but in my pain I see You're moulding me, You are the Potter, I'm the clay. In Your hands, for every storm there's a reason, In Your hands, there's a time for every season, though my tears fall, you hold me close, love me through it all, in Your hands. You turn my weeping into dancing, You give my feet a place to stand, You will not turn away the asking, even when your ways are hard to understand.*'[2]

October 16th – Andy and Jennifer

We got this text from a very good friend and want to share it, as we feel it sums up why we can stay positive, and why we don't doubt that Oliver is going to be just fine no matter what it takes to get us to that point:

> '*I've just read your post on Oliver's Blog. Reading it made me feel so sad because it's not the news we were all wanting to hear. But then I read the words of*

---

[2] Song 'In Your Hands' [Kelly Minter and Rick Heil] © copyright 2001 Word Music.

the song you quoted and I realised that by me thinking that, I was somehow thinking I knew best (that surgery now would be the most ideal thing) but God's the potter, not us and He's NOT just fumbling his way through this – He has a masterplan and He's working on that every single day. I can't begin to understand this plan and I can't imagine the turmoil and pain you must have in your hearts, but I will continue to pray that while God continues to work, you would be able to know, and trust, that Oliver's life is in the hands of the almighty and all powerful God, who knows more than anyone what is best for Oliver, and for whom nothing is impossible.'

So Far, So Good

TIME PASSED SO much more quickly than we ever expected it would. Now we wish it had not. At the start, thirty weeks sounded like a lifetime, but with everything we had to get used to and deal with, time just flew by. Oliver got off to a great start with his treatment, and amazed everyone with how well he coped. He was expected to be a very sickly baby and was not expected to be able to get out very often.

Ward 2 – the oncology ward at Sick Kids, is surprisingly a very happy place. Oliver's consultant Mark and the staff are amazing and the sense of hope and positivity is strong. They not only cared for Oliver, they cared for us too. We spent so much time with them that they became like a new family for us during the weeks of treatment.

People were very kind to us at the hospital and the CLIC House was very handy. The consultants made it sound like a bonus whenever Oliver could stay there with us instead of on the ward, but nothing stopped us being desperate to get to our own home. The consultants were well aware of this and knew that whenever they asked if we had any questions, 'When are we getting home?' was always pretty high on our list. While we knew Oliver needed to be in hospital to be treated, we still longed for time at home with him as a normal family. When we were at home it was easy to forget that there was anything wrong because he was developing normally, looking so healthy and smiling his way through.

High temperatures in children with cancer are taken very seriously. If they get an infection they can get very ill very quickly. This is why the consultants were so strict about Oliver being on the ward or at CLIC when his counts were low. He was so little that if he did get a high temperature he would need antibiotics as soon as possible. It was a miracle that Oliver did not get many high temperatures and we are very thankful for this.

We always loved having Oliver at home and going back to Edinburgh was always hard. We would be told to bring a 'just in case' bag for having to stay if counts were low. Our 'just in case' bag was actually a 'just in case' car load, and whether we were having to stay for two days or all week, we always needed the same amount of stuff. We would pack our 'just in case car load' every day forevermore if it meant having Oliver here with us. We moaned at the time, but we yearn for it now.

We were always told that curing Oliver would be difficult, but all the feedback we received was positive. We were continually told by the medics that they were treating him to cure him. They were treating the tumour so it would go away and never come back. We were told that because they knew the treatment was working on the main tumour (and had already eradicated a much smaller lump on his groin) it would also be working everywhere else, so the cancer would not be spreading. We were always so encouraged by all this feedback, and right from the start were counting down the days to taking our baby home for good. We were told over and over that Oliver was doing better than anyone could have expected. The frustrating thing is that he was!

Oliver impressed the medical staff with how well he responded to and coped with treatment, but he also amazed them with how he continued to thrive throughout treatment – growing and developing perfectly normally as well as feeding well, being very alert for his stage, and being extremely chilled out about everything. We were often told that the reason Oliver was so calm was because we were so calm and positive. We were calm and positive because we had a vast and constantly growing army of people praying for us across the world. We've made a list of all the countries we have received messages from about Oliver, twenty-three in total. This meant we had round the clock prayer and we certainly experienced the benefits of this.

We were so well supported during our time with Oliver. We had two churches as well as family and friends providing us with all our meals, which was such a practical way of helping and a real blessing. We would never leave Oliver alone, so when he was on the ward one of us would be able to nip over to the CLIC house to heat up meals to bring back to the ward. Granny Black had just retired in the summer, which was perfect timing for her to be able to be there with us and for us. Andy had to go back to work but it meant Granny Black could be in Edinburgh to help, and she and Andy would swap over at weekends.

Once we got over the initial disappointment of surgery not being possible at week twelve, we regained our positive mindsets and entered week thirteen full of hope. We were confident it would all work out and were confident that God was at work in our lives in ways we did not understand. Oliver helped us massively with his huge smile, priceless cuddles, sparkly eyes and love of life. He was blissfully unaware of all that was happening, and just made the most of every day. Week thirty still felt like ages away but everything was going so well, and we were almost half way through treatment. We were even now being told about what would happen once treatment was finished – the central line being removed, regular check-ups well into adulthood and being allowed to finally take our baby home forever and get on with 'normal' family life.

Weeks 13–24

October 16th – Oliver

For the first time in my whole life I've just met someone smaller than I am! I felt so grown up when we went to visit friends to meet their new baby who was born last week. I look forward to playing with her and teaching her about important things, like monkeys.

Introducing my new best friend Amos

Another thing I'm looking forward to is going to see Abi tomorrow, because it will be the first time I will have been to Edinburgh without going to hospital! Granny and Grandpa Black bought me a new monkey who I've named Amos so I'll take him with me. I've started making some new noises and I quite like the look of the TV but Mummy and Daddy keep turning me away from it!

We now have cushions to match our sofas which Mummy is very happy about. Daddy and I don't see what the big deal is but Daddy says it's best to agree. Daddy is making the dinner just now and then we're going to have a relaxing evening. I like to stay up late and have a long lie-in in the morning (with a couple of milk breaks) then I sleep as little as possible during the day because I don't like to miss anything.

October 20th – Oliver

Week 13 – done! Well, the hospital part of it is anyway! We got told to come in late morning on Monday and we managed to arrive at 11.55 am! Chemo didn't start till 3.30 pm though so it was fine. I got a good cuddle from Honorary Auntie Kate, Auntie Catherine read me my new story book and Honorary Auntie Catriona brought us our dinner, so I had a good day and was home by tea-time yesterday.

After keeping Mummy awake during the night at the hospital I thought I should be nice last night so I slept for seven hours, then I was awake for one hour, then back to sleep for three hours so hopefully that made up for it. My consultant said if he'd been told in July I'd be doing this well now he would not have believed it.

I had a nice visit to Abi's on Sunday. I think I might have found out what a 'pinch' is although maybe I just cried cos I was made to sit beside a girl! I hadn't seen Uncle Alasdair for a while either. I think he's shrunk, but maybe it's more that I've grown! Going back to my toys now ...

October 21st – Oliver

After my last wall post I realised that week thirteen has been a bit quick and uneventful so I started thinking of how to change that. I thought through all the hospital services that are available to try out. MRI? Check. CT Scan? Check. X-ray? Check. Ultrasound? Check. Physio? Check. Chemo? Check. Theatre? Check. A&E? Hmm – interesting. I warmed up just enough for the hospital to want to check me over, so as soon as Daddy got in from work, off we went! The nurses at A&E were wondering why I was so smiley. Well I was just joking about the high temperature. I didn't think they were going to take it seriously! They wanted to be cautious though, so off to my ward we went and stayed the night, but first thing this morning they were happy to let me home again. Having tried out A&E I'd be happy to never go there again, so please pray that I won't have to!

October 27th – Oliver

I'm using Mummy's phone just now to do a quick update as we're in Edinburgh this week and my laptop cable has broken (Daddy has ordered me a new one so I'll hopefully get it soon). My counts are low so they're keeping a close eye on me at the hospital but I'll hopefully have most of next week at home. Daddy's coming to visit tonight. I can't wait to see him. I've recently discovered something called mirrors. They make me smile because I see a very smiley baby looking at me. He looks like good fun! Will write more soon ...

October 29th – Oliver

I've spent two nights on the ward but now that I'm my happy little self again I get to go to CLIC tonight and hopefully my counts will be up in time to go home on Monday. My Daddy is a maths teacher so he's good at counting. He'll be here for the weekend so that will definitely help me! I'm using Mummy's phone again but I'll write more when I have my laptop back. Just thought I'd say a quick hello and let you know I'm doing well. At the end of next week I'll be half way through treatment! We can now see the light at the end of the tunnel – to Daddy they are just normal and very good lights, but to Mummy they are fireworks at Disneyland! Apparently we only go to Disneyland once though, so I think I should wait till I'm old enough to appreciate it! I believe everything Daddy tells me! Talk to you again soon ...

Our shoes – aren't mine tiny?!

October 30th - Andy and Jennifer

This week we had two unexpected nights on the ward while Oliver's counts were very low and he wasn't quite himself. His consultant said he's been doing so surprisingly well so far, that they don't want to take any chances. He is now back to his normal chilled out happy self, and counts are on the way back up, in time for hopefully going home on Monday for a week before being on the ward for five days.

Please continue to pray for him and for the decisions being made just now regarding surgery – where and how it will be done, who will do it and when it will happen.

His consultants said they will work exhaustively to find the best possible option. We asked one of them this week just how rare Oliver's case is – one in a million? He said it's unique! This is why they really don't know all the answers, and are just so pleased to see how well Oliver is doing so far.

We're enjoying our weekend together and will pop into Oliver's Auntie Catherine's 21st birthday ceilidh tonight. She is very kindly asking for donations for CLIC instead of gifts for herself. Oliver will enjoy an evening with Granny and Grandpa Black!

November 2nd - Oliver

Well Daddy's counting skills definitely helped me as I'm now home again, and all going well it will be till next Monday. This gives me lots of time to hang out in my own house! I had a huge dilemma with what to do with the extra hour when the clocks changed on Sunday – play or sleep or play or sleep. I was thinking play, Mummy and Daddy were thinking sleep. I spent so long trying to decide that I ended up sleeping! Late morning I slept for an extra hour and a bit when I'd normally just sleep for the bit! I had a nice visit from Auntie Jo and Granny Gill today. I haven't seen Auntie Jo for ages, so I was able to show her how big I am now, how smiley I am, and I took her upstairs to see my cool bedroom. The plan for the rest of the week is to have lots of fun at home, with no high temperatures or reasons for going to Edinburgh, so please pray that plan works!

Pyjama morning and Mummy cuddles = happy me!

November 5th – Oliver

Good news is I'm still at home and I got called a 'medical marvel' by one of my nurses today, so I'm quite proud of that. I've had a fun week at home playing with my toys in my room. There has been so much to see and do that I've decided to cut down my sleeping hours. Daddy will appreciate this now that it's the weekend. He'll get to be up with me during the night! I've also discovered the answer to shopping – fall asleep in the car then Daddy or Granny will sit with me in the car so I don't get disturbed while Mummy gets what we need. We went curtain shopping yesterday – I mean – come on!! Toy shopping I do, any other shopping I do not do!

I have a few visitors lined up for the weekend and I'll hopefully make it out to church on Sunday before I pack up for another week in Edinburgh. I'll have lots to tell my friends at the hospital. Oh and I'm now half way through my treatment – week 16 here I come!!

November 6th – Andy and Jennifer

We have enjoyed a week at home with Oliver, and ask that you continue to pray for him as he starts five days of treatment on Monday. He will be in hospital Monday to Saturday. It's annoying that home times pass so quickly ... but then Edinburgh times do too. All the time we are getting closer to being home for good, and we cannot wait!

We still await news about surgery but are in no doubt that Oliver's consultants will find the best possible option for him, and that all of this will soon be behind us. It is crazy to think we are now half way through!

Me with the proudest parents in the world

Obviously it's horrible to see Oliver having to go through all this, but at the same time it is wonderful to see how well he is coping and developing, and how amazing his smile is throughout. He is one of the happiest, most chilled out babies ever! We are loving being his parents, and are so blessed and privileged to have him. We are experiencing and learning so many things which we would never have thought we could cope with if we'd known in advance all of this was going to happen. However, we know that God is using all of this to shape and strengthen us in ways that we cannot even imagine.

Please pray that the second half of treatment goes as well as the first and that Oliver continues to respond so well, remain so happy, develop so normally, as well as impress and amaze everyone involved in his treatment.

11th November – Oliver

My week is going well and Daddy came last night to stay till we go home on Saturday so that's pretty cool. He slept on the ward with me. Mummy was gutted that I only woke up once for him after my previous two nights' efforts! I was quite crabby on Monday and Tuesday. They say it could be due to some of the medicine I'm on, but the truth is I was just happy being at home so not pleased to be back here.

As we're getting closer to Saturday though I'm getting much more smiley! Being here is not so bad really. I'm constantly getting told how gorgeous and clever I am! I've reached over 14lbs in weight now so that's quite exciting, and I got a new pair of jeans to celebrate my four month birthday.

Mummy and Daddy have been a bit upset about something the surgeon said but they said lots of good things too, and they shouldn't worry cos whatever happens I'm still going to be smiley, cheeky and lots of fun!

Andy and Jennifer

We've had quite a tough week as far as finding out about surgeons and their tactfulness! On Monday we found out that Oliver's consultants have decided that the sooner he has surgery, the better. The surgeons have said they'll cancel whatever else they need to once a date is decided for Oliver's surgery.

He had an ultrasound on Monday which showed that the tumour has not shrunk any further since the MRI, and they do not want to give it any chance to grow again considering how quickly it grew in the first place. Therefore, although not confirmed yet, surgery is likely to be during the week beginning November 29th. Surgery is complex for many reasons and they won't know what they're faced with until Oliver is in theatre.

The two surgeons yesterday were fairly positive about things but today's surgeon said to us that if they can't take all the tumour out they 'could go for a more radical option, and by that I mean removing his arm'. Naturally we were quite shocked and upset by this, but were also reassured by Oliver's consultants that while they do need to listen to the surgeons, it is also definitely not on their own agenda for Oliver. Ideally, it would be fantastic if they could remove all of the tumour but this is unlikely due to its size and position. The other option is to remove as much of it as possible and let chemo deal with the rest – this is what Oliver's consultants are planning for and are positive about. They have, however, said that if removing his arm was definitely the only hope of a cure for Oliver, then it would be a last resort, and a difficult decision we'd have to think about. We've certainly been given plenty to pray about!

One of the songs that often plays on a CD on our many trips to and from Edinburgh includes the words:

> '*Do you believe me if I say God can make miracles happen today? Do you believe me if I say you don't need to wait for an answer before you step out in faith?*'[1]

[1] Words and music by Marty Sampson - copyright 2002 Marty Sampson/Hillsong Publishing

Well, yes we do believe God can make miracles happen today. And as it's something we have been thinking about for a while, we both feel it is time we stepped out in faith and asked you all to pray for a miracle for Oliver. Obviously we want what is best for him, and as no one seems to have answers just now we don't know what a miracle means for Oliver. It could be that they find they are able to remove all of the tumour, or that this week's chemo has made it smaller, or that what we are seeing is dead tissue, or that they are able to take out most of it and chemo gets rid of the rest. It could mean he has no, some or all use of his arm. We really don't know, but we do rely on and value your prayers for Oliver, and trust that God is in complete control. He is able to do infinitely more than we can ever ask or hope for. He can use these surgeons in ways they don't even yet know, and can continue to help Oliver to respond to and cope with treatment in ways that no one expects. Please all join with our family in praying for a miracle for Oliver as surgery is now only a couple of weeks away.

November 13th - Oliver

Just thought I'd let you know where I am right now – relaxing on my couch at my house with my Mummy and Daddy with a bottle of milk within reach. It doesn't get much better than that!

You'll never guess what's happened – the doses of my medicines have increased cos I've put on weight!!! However, I've discovered that holding my bottom lip in tightly is a pretty effective way of keeping medicine out! The good thing is that because I'm coping so well with treatment I've been given fewer medicines to come home with. (My Granny Black will be so proud of me knowing the difference between 'less' and 'fewer' already!)

My nurse came into my room this morning. CBeebies was on TV, Mummy was playing with my new frog puppet while I was fast asleep on Daddy's knee. Man, I'm only four months old and they're an embarrassment to me already!

Our main discovery this week was that we don't like surgeons, but we are sure that they are good at their job, and that together with God and my consultants they will make me better. Anyway, I'm meant to be watching the rugby with Daddy just now so I'd better get back to it. I don't quite see what the fuss is about but he assures me I'll learn to love it!

15th November – Oliver

We went to church last night and you'll never guess what the sermon was about...My monkey, Amos!! Well, I thought it was, and Mummy had to stop me from holding up Amos who I was playing with at the time when the minister asked, 'Has anyone found Amos in the Bible?'! Turns out there is more than one Amos. Everyone was very impressed with how well I look and how smiley I am. Mummy and Daddy would like me to give you a big prayer request for tomorrow ... I'm getting a couple of scans at 11 am-ish to help plan for surgery which means fasting (eek) from 8 am and being in Edinburgh for 9 am-ish. Prayers really helped me last time to forget I was hungry so we're hoping for the same again! I'll also be hanging out in Edinburgh for the rest of the week before hopefully having most of next week at home.

17th November – Oliver

I did some more impressing people with how well I managed to fast – didn't even cry once! I fed at 6.15 am then went back to sleep. Mummy woke me at 8 am to feed me again before fasting, but I was still half asleep and had forgotten about the whole fasting thing so wouldn't take it! I felt so stupid once I realised! Then, we got a flat tyre which seemed like a bad thing at first, but it meant I spent more of the fasting time asleep in the car, so it worked out well!

Once at hospital so many people were coming to talk to me that I was quite distracted from my empty tummy. I also realised that dummies are actually quite good even though I'd stopped liking them lately. I got taken at 12.30 for my MRI and CT scans and was back to the world of milk at 2 pm. My consultant said they normally keep kids in till they're feeding well again but that's not a problem for me! Too right! We should get scan results and surgery plans tomorrow so Daddy is coming after work today to stay. Will let you know when we do ...

18th November – Andy and Jennifer

A week ago when we asked you to pray for a miracle we didn't know what that meant. Now we do. Today we met with Oliver's consultant expecting plans for surgery, but instead our world was turned upside down. He said that Tuesday's scans show that the tumour has grown and so they aren't willing to operate. He also said that the cancer has spread to Oliver's lungs – chemo is not working any longer and radiotherapy is too much for him. This has come as a huge shock to us all, including his consultants. We have never been overly positive on the blog – everything has been positive. Oliver has been coping very well with treatment at the same time as growing and developing normally and smiling his way through.

Please EVERYONE pray for a miracle and ask everyone you know to do the same. We don't know if it will happen but we do believe in a God for whom nothing is impossible. This is not over yet and we refuse to even begin to try to accept that it is, unless we know that we have done everything we can for our gorgeous Oliver. We don't just sound desperate, we are desperate. We need everyone to pray and to pray hard. To many of you we might sound crazy, but this is what we believe, and we know that if it is in God's plan it can and will happen.

20th November - Oliver

I haven't written for a while so thought I'd say hey! Yesterday I had my last visit to Ward 2. I was a bit bored so I tried to do two of my favourite things at the same time – smiling and feeding. It turns out it's not easy – but I like doing them both so much that I couldn't decide which to stop doing!

I get to be at home all the time – we're staying with Granny and Grandpa Black and Granny Gill is here too. This means I am getting loads of attention, cuddles and people to play with. I'm amazed at how many friends I have on here on Facebook, and thank you so much for all your messages. Remember the frog song I once told you about? *Fully Rely On God ... cos He can do ANYTHING!* Gotta believe it!

22nd November - Andy and Jennifer

We are now at home with Oliver and his huge smile and rosy cheeks make it very hard to believe that this is all really happening. We are so, so grateful for everyone's prayers and encouragement, and are amazed that our four month old baby has been able to touch so many hearts in such a short time. It was so hard leaving the hospital at the end of last week – the staff and families there have become so much part of our lives in the last few months, and the chemo was always meant to cure Oliver. Now we are left without the hope of the treatment to cure him, but we do still have the much greater hope of our unchanging and ever-faithful God.

Oliver amazed everyone with how well he coped with treatment. He was expected to lose weight, need tube feeding and be a sickly baby but none of that happened. He is a strong baby and already at four months is being used by God in ways that we don't understand but do trust in. He loves Oliver more than we do (which must be A LOT!!) and has him safe in His loving hands.

Please keep praying for a miracle for Oliver that he will be with us for a long time to come, and be able to share his already amazing life story for God's glory.

*Mr Monkey is just the coolest
and is even on my bedroom wall!*

24th November – Oliver

Yesterday was a day of firsts – Grandpa Gill changed my nappy, I became the proud owner of a bowl and spoon, I tried baby rice and I used my bouncy swing! The idea behind the rice was to help me sleep longer at night. I did an oopsy though and forgot all about this! Daddy's side of the family are very into maths so naturally numbers are in my system. I was dreaming of even numbers last night and so fed at 2, 4, 6 and 8. I don't have many medicines to take anymore – hurray! There is one that I have to take today though, so I'm pretending to be asleep each time I hear it mentioned. I used to get the kids' version which tasted like banana – but I felt I was getting too big for kids' medicine so stopped taking it. Now I have the adult version which tastes like aniseed – yuck!! Oh oh, time to 'sleep' again ...

26th November – Andy and Jennifer

When Oliver's consultant was telling us last week that the tumour had grown, the cancer had spread and that curing him was no longer possible, we listened, cried and felt we had to believe what he was saying – after all, he's the consultant. Then we realised we could still ask God for a miracle – the doctors may be helpless, but our God is not. If it is in His will, we know He can and will heal Oliver, and the overwhelming response to Oliver's Blog over the last week has further confirmed to us that we can and should be praying for a miracle. Oliver has amazed the medics so far and we hope and pray he will continue to do so. He's so happy, chilled out and healthy looking that it is often hard to believe that any of this is actually real. We have to talk to people involved in the medical side, and make decisions for how they're expecting things to go. At the same time we are holding onto our hope in Jesus and urgently and desperately praying for healing.

A week ago home was the last place we wanted to be after months of being desperate to be at home. Packing, unpacking, living out of bags and loading the 'just in case' car load every other day didn't quite seem so bad anymore. The Hospital–home–CLIC routine had become our life and it is strange to think it is over.

A week ago we also never thought we'd be able to talk to anyone again without our eyes filling up, and we never thought we'd be able to keep entertaining and caring for Oliver as he needs us to. Your hundreds of comments and continued prayers are definitely helping us as a family. One week on we are enjoying quality family time in our own house and enjoying being able to go out and about. We're also feeling a lot more positive about everything and are holding tightly onto God's promises, which so many of you have been highlighting on the blog this week.

Please continue to pray for Oliver. It's not known what's expected or the timescale of things that are expected. Please pray he doesn't experience pain or discomfort, he continues to feed as well as he has always done, (even if this does mean two hourly at night!!), that we are able to stay strong and happy for him, that he keeps smiling and that God will be at work in his little body, healing him from this awful illness – it seems impossible to us, but with God all things are possible. When Oliver was up during the night last night a song that came to mind was this kids' song:

> *'Sometimes I feel afraid, of things I cannot see, of monsters in the dark that might be chasing after me ... but then I remember, there's no need to be afraid ... because my God He is big, He's gigantic, He's enormous, He is powerful and strong, He's amazing and He's awesome and there's NOTHING in this world that He couldn't pulverise, so I know I've got nothing to fear, no, no, no I know I've got nothing to fear.'[2]*

November 28th – Oliver

I was SO excited when I looked out of my bedroom window this morning. Everything had turned into milk and there was even milk falling from the sky. It was like a dream come true! Then Daddy went outside and made a milkman for me, and a milkbaby too! I've since found out that it's not actually milk, it's something called snow. Once I got over the disappointment of it not being milk, I realised it's actually quite fun. I'm really enjoying being home. I have so many fun things to do and my grannies and grandpas have been visiting me, as well as my Auntie Catherine and (hopefully

---

[2] *Sometimes I feel afraid* by Joe Hemming and Nigel Hemming, © copyright 2001 Vineyard songs (U.K. Eire). Use by permission.

My garden covered in milk!
(I later found out it was actually something called 'snow')

future Uncle) Chris. I'm finding the words 'boo' and 'keek' more funny than ever.

Something I didn't find funny was when I punched myself in the face the other night. It brought real tears to my eyes. I'm over it now though, don't worry. We're having a cosy day at home today just the three of us – lovin' it! I was kind to Mummy and Daddy last night – I slept for three whole hours in between two of my feeds. I didn't quite manage three the rest of the time.

November 30th - Oliver

Mummy never thought I'd be able to use the following words in the same sentence, but ... My Uncle Alasdair is well cool! Not only did he join Facebook just for me (Mummy and Auntie Esther didn't manage to convince him!) but he also took today off work so he could come see me with Auntie Esther and cousin Abi. All the milk on the roads didn't put them off! I reckon this must mean I'm well cool too.

Cousin Abi was eating lots of interesting looking things – far more interesting than silly baby rice!! We played in my room for a while but then I got a bit tired and fell asleep (that's what happens when you don't sleep much at night!) Now I'm hanging out with Mummy and Daddy, keeping cosy, reading 'That's Not My Penguin', singing songs and playing with all my toys.

December 2nd - Andy and Jennifer

Today we were told of the things that might happen to Oliver and the things that are expected to happen. So we just want to put an update on here to say how desperately and urgently we need everyone to pray for a miracle in Oliver's little body and life. No medical treatment anywhere in the world could cure him. We have had several ideas suggested to us this week but with everything stripped away we really know what it is to be fully relying on God and His mercy. Medically, Oliver is expected to have a few months maximum, and while we ask you to pray against all the things that could happen to him, we ultimately ask you all to pray for this miracle, that Oliver will be healed and that his life will glorify God in every way possible. His tumour has visibly grown over the last week but he is still smiling and isn't in pain. It's a very hard and uncertain time with a situation that seems impossible to fix, but it's definitely not over yet and all things are possible with God.

I just can't stop smiling!

December 3rd – Oliver

Baby rice – are you kidding!? Sweet Potato Bake and Pear and Apple Pudding, washed down with mummy milk – now you're talking!! The idea behind it all is to get me to sleep longer at night. Again, are you kidding!? I just can't help myself. I did try my hardest last night. I made it to just over three hours in one go, but then I had to give up and wake Mummy and Daddy. To me it was three hours, to them it was less because apparently I wriggle and breath quite heavily for quite a while before I wake up. (I see this as a good thing because they're ready to feed and change me by the time I do actually wake up. Sometimes I even manage to feed and go back to sleep without even opening my eyes!) I don't see the problem with night and day being much the same thing. Mummy and Daddy don't seem to see my point though. I had all my grandparents here today so I was showing off how strong my legs are by kicking them in the air lots. It's been a good day.

December 6th – Andy and Jennifer

Oliver continues to be his happy, hungry little self. We're very thankful he has not experienced pain or any other things we've been told are possible. We ask you to pray this continues. Seeing his tumour now looking so big is scary, but we keep reminding ourselves that it may be big, but God is bigger. We're constantly and desperately praying and pleading for a miracle, and while we think, if it's going to happen, it should be now, we also have to remind ourselves that God's timing is perfect. A song we quoted a while back still rings true:

> *'... in my pain I see You're moulding me, You are the Potter, I'm the clay ... You turn my weeping into dancing, You give my feet a place to stand, You will not turn away the asking, even when Your ways are hard to understand. In Your hands, for every storm there's a reason ...'.*[a]

Me and my Mummy

---

[a] Song 'In Your Hands' [Kelly Minter and Rick Heil] © copyright 2001 Word Music.

Please keep praying for Oliver. We love him so much and are thankful for every minute with him. We long and hope to be able to put an update on here one day to say he has been healed ... for now though, please keep praying.

TRYING to teach Daddy how to look good in photos

Oliver

Hi! I've been told I have to be quick cos it's bedtime (he he). We had a pj day today. I like pj days, especially when going out these days means having to wear ski suits that are impossible to move in!

We went for a walk yesterday and I do apologise, but I kept blinking when the camera flashed so the photos are no good. I will try to convince Mummy to put up a funny video of her and me dancing though.

The snow stopped anyone coming to see me today so it's just been the three of us. Daddy had to walk to the supermarket because I was running out of nappies and that's not a good thing to run out of. Anyway, it's all sorted now. I've worked out how to make my squeaky toys squeak so I'm having lots of fun with that. Mummy and

Daddy think it's great ... for now! Right, better go try to sleep. It's only two hours till my next feed!

December 10th - Oliver

Happy 5 monthirthday to me! (I made up that word by the way!) Talking about words, 'ping' is my new favourite – even better than 'keek' or 'boo'. It has to be said in a high pitched voice and you have to close your eyes and open them as you say it. That's all I ask and I find it incredibly funny. So I'm getting a bit confused – last week there was milk falling from the sky and making everything look like milk, and now we have a tree in our sitting room. It's like everything gets turned inside out at this time of year!

Our sitting room is looking very cosy with lots of Christmas lights. We were sorting through all the clothes that are too wee for me now. I can't believe I ever fitted the 0–3 months ones. Mummy can't believe I got big enough for the 3–6 months ones cos they looked so big when I got them!

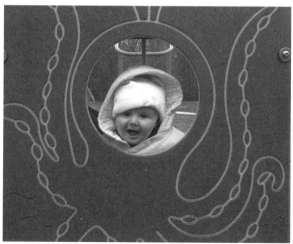

Having fun being an octopus!

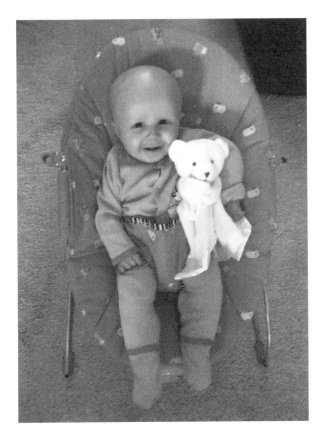

I think I'm going to need a bigger bouncy chair soon!

We have a busy weekend planned so hopefully there will be no more of that milk/snow stuff so we can do all we want to do.

December 11th - Andy and Jennifer

We've had a lovely day Christmas shopping and out for coffee in St Andrews after lunch with Oliver's Great-Auntie Maggie. We're so grateful Oliver is still his happy, healthy looking self and is not in any pain. Please pray this continues. Again, the tumour is looking bigger but again, God is still bigger. No matter how big it may get, God will still be bigger and that is why we have hope. We continue to plead for the miracle of healing in Oliver's little body. Granny and Grandpa Black babysat last night while we went to see the Narnia film at the cinema. Our minds were more focused on praying for Oliver, but one quote stood out:

> '*Sometimes extraordinary things happen to extraordinary people, and their destiny can be more extraordinary than they can imagine.*'[4]

Well, we think Oliver is pretty extraordinary so far and it made us think of this verse:

> '*Now all glory to God , who is able, through his mighty power at work within us, to accomplish infinitely more than we might ask or think*' (Eph. 3:20).

Please continue to pray.

December 14th - Oliver

I had my first trip to St Andrews on Saturday. We planned to go to the Sea Life Centre but it's closed while they work on their meercat enclosure. I may only be five months old but even I know meercats are not sea life! We went Christmas shopping and for coffee instead.

Now that we don't have to worry about blood counts I can actually go into shops. Daddy and I felt this was the down side, but we ended up having a fun time seeing all the Christmassy things. I didn't want to feel left out when we went for coffee, so I took my milk with me.

---

[4] Words from film: Voyage of the Dawn Treader. © copyright DISNEY ENTERPRISES, INC. and WALDEN MEDIA, LLC. All rights reserved.

Hanging out with Santa

Yesterday I surprised Granny Gill for her birthday by arriving at her door when she thought she was coming to my house!

My nurses came today and were very impressed with how well I look and how happy I am despite all that's going on and what could be happening.

I've even managed to sleep for up to four hours at night – with the help of a dummy. I suck dummies very loudly though so I'm not sure Mummy and Daddy are benefiting much from the extra sleepage!

December 15th – Andy and Jennifer

It has now been four weeks since we were told the devastating news that Oliver's cancer had spread and is incurable. Four weeks on,

Oliver is continuing to surprise everyone with how well he is and looks and how big his smiles continue to be. Four weeks on, we are remaining positive and holding onto the Hope that nobody can take away from us.

We are constantly praying for the miracle of healing and that for many years to come Oliver will continue to bring joy to our lives and glory to God. The tumour grew significantly a few weeks ago but since then the rate of growth appears to have slowed down. It still looks very big. We are so thankful that he is not bothered by any of this and that he is not in pain, please pray this continues.

We pray so much that God will shrink this tumour and heal Oliver of all the cancer in his body. Medically it's impossible but we know He has the power to do this and plead that He does. We are so grateful for all your prayers and ask you to continue to plead for healing in Oliver's life.

December 17th – Oliver

I've been doing quite a bit of thinking about sleeping and I feel four hours in one go is just too much – who knows what I might be missing – so I've limited myself to two to three hours again and am much happier with this. Also, I was lying in my cot gazing at Mummy and Daddy's bed and thinking how much more comfy it looked. So, early this morning, I cried and Mummy lay me on their bed just for a second to give me my dummy, but I took my chance and fell asleep and oh it was a good sleep. I knew Mummy and Daddy wouldn't want to move me when I was looking soooo comfy, even though I'd positioned myself in the most awkward place possible for anyone else to fit on the bed, but we cuddled up and managed! We went to Deep Sea World this week and I got Mummy to take a photo to prove I found Nemo. Then we went to buy my Santa stocking. My cousin Donald from Stornoway came to visit me and took us out for lunch, then I was out again for lunch yesterday. Not having to worry about blood counts is great. I'm such a busy boy these days!

*Just one week before Christmas,
in my new Christmas pyjamas*

Andy and Jennifer

The potential of what the tumour can do is frightening. The power of God and what He can do is exciting. The sight of the tumour seems to bring the temptation to think that Oliver can't possibly get better, but we know all things are possible with God, and every time we see it we remind ourselves that God is so much bigger than it.

Oliver's smile many times throughout each day reminds us that there is definitely still hope. His hair is now growing back in, as are his eyebrows and eyelashes – signs of new life and so lovely to see.

We pray so hard, and what feels like every second of every day, that in His love, power and mercy God will completely heal Oliver, and we ask you to do the same. We already see many ways in which God has been at work in this whole journey – and we wait with hope and confidence, knowing that Oliver is completely safe in His hands.

December 21st – Andy and Jennifer

We'd just like to ask everyone to pray for Oliver this afternoon as he has not been himself for the last couple of days – very sleepy and irritable – which as you know from his photos and updates is definitely not like him! His body is coping with a lot but we'd just like to see him back to his happy, playful self. It could be related to the cancer, or it could be a normal baby thing as teething is certainly one of the things bothering him just now. The tumour is still looking horribly big and we just keep praying that God's goodness will overcome this evil. Please pray this passes and of course, as always, please pray for healing.

Yesterday morning we prayed for encouragement and while Oliver was going through a happier phase playing in his cot, we noticed a small rainbow out of his bedroom window. It reminded us of 'The Lessons Learned from Noah's Ark', the last of which is, 'no matter the storm, when you're with God, there's always a rainbow waiting'. Please pray Oliver's rainbow comes soon.

December 22nd – Andy and Jennifer

Please everyone pray for Oliver today. There is a big change today – he's very pale, sick and sleepy. Please pray he will be free from pain. It's never too late for God to heal and this is our ultimate prayer. Please all pray. The nurses are here and the consultant is on his way. God is still in control.

Love Andy, Jennifer and Oliver

Andy and Jennifer

Today has been so hard. Seeing Oliver so pale, sick and sleeping so much is so painful. We really do believe God can heal Oliver, it's not too late, and we pray so desperately that He does. 'Humanly speaking it is impossible. But with God everything is possible' (Matt. 19:26). If Oliver is not going to be healed our prayer is that he will not have to suffer. He's a little fighter though and it's not over yet. We are so encouraged by so many people praying and appreciate all your messages. We know God can still turn this around and bring light to the darkness, but we trust Him no matter what. Please keep praying.

'And though my heart is torn, I'll praise You in this storm'.[5]

December 23rd – Andy and Jennifer

Just a quick update. We have been up all night with Oliver as we've been told it could be a matter of minutes, hours or maybe days. Oliver is very peacefully enjoying constant cuddles and is sleeping most of the time. It is so, so painful to be going through this, and so while we still pray for a miracle, knowing that all things are possible, we're also praying he will not have to suffer any pain.

---

[5] Words and music by Marty Sampson. © 2002 Marty Sampson/Hillsong Publishing.

> 'Abba, Father', he cried out, 'everything is possible for
> you. Please take the cup of suffering away from me. Yet
> I want your will to be done, not mine' (Mark 14:36).

December 24th – Andy and Jennifer

This morning we cuddled Oliver in our bed telling him how much we loved him, and how amazing he is, as his breathing slowed down and it seemed he was being taken Home. We prayed for God to take him quickly to put an end to this suffering. Shortly after, his breathing improved and although he is sleeping due to medication he is still with us.

A doctor who was meeting him for the first time came and said he doesn't know how things will progress, because from what he's heard from the other doctors, this little guy doesn't stick to the rules! His breathing is good and his heart is strong.

We then did our daily Bible reading. We're randomly using May's as we don't have the ones for this month. The 24th's reading was about Peter and John and how it's never too late for healing! It asked if you know anyone who needs healing, and talked about looking in the eyes of suffering.

We've had such a sense of peace today and are feeling the most positive we have felt all week. When Oliver has opened his eyes we've been singing songs and showing him his toys. We've always said that while he's still here there is still hope, and he is still here so there is still hope! Please do continue to pray for healing, and at the same time that if that isn't what is to happen, that he will be freed from pain.

December 25th

Thank you all for your faithfulness in praying for Oliver and for us. He is thankfully no longer in pain and went quickly and peacefully this morning, cuddled up to us in his favourite position – left shoulder, not right!

None of us could have kept going, it got too hard and so we are thankful that he is free from all of this. We will never understand why all this has been allowed to happen to our gorgeous boy, but we will keep trusting. We still believe in a God who could have healed Oliver, but for some reason chose not to. We trust that somehow this is a good reason. We are also very aware of how He has provided for us and looked after us for the last five and a half months, carrying us through sufficiently.

We don't really know what else to say, but we are thankful for, and amazed at the lasting impression Oliver's fantastic smile and love of life have made across the world. It was quite a journey we were on but are so thankful for the time we had with him, and so privileged that we were blessed with such a beautiful, happy baby to love and look after. For now it's hard to see how we'll ever get through the pain, but we know that one day we will be with him again forever, in a place free from suffering. Please continue to pray for strength and peace for us and our families.

Thank you all again,

Love Andy and Jennifer

'And as the thunder rolls

I barely hear You whisper through the rain

'I'm with you'

And as Your mercy falls

I raise my hands to praise the God

Who gives and takes away

I'll praise You in this storm

I will raise my hands

For You are who You are

No matter where I am

And every tear I've cried

You hold in Your hands

And though my heart is torn

I will praise you in this storm'.[8]

---

[8] Praise you in this storm by Casting Crowns. Published by Small Stone Media, Netherlands, sub-publisher of EMI Music.

Darling Oliver

WE WROTE THIS letter to Oliver. It was read out at his funeral service by Gill Deaves, one of Oliver's nurses. We also gave him the hand written version to take with him. We feel it summarises our story and expresses our love for our baby, and our heartache of losing him.

Darling Oliver

No words can express how much we love and miss you, just as no words can help ease our pain just now. You had exactly 24 weeks to make your mark on the world and you sure managed to do that in style.

It seems no coincidence that you were due on your Daddy's birthday, diagnosed on your Mummy's birthday, called Home on Christmas Day and have people come to celebrate your little life on New Year's Eve. We would never have forgotten you anyway, and now no one else will either. You were also showing maths was in your genes from a very young age – you were born at 10 to 7, passed away at 10 past 7 and your birth date was 10/7/10.

You first let us see your beautiful smile when you were only two weeks old – sooner than most babies, but you were just so happy you couldn't seem to help it. We loved how, when we looked into your cot in the morning, the first thing you'd do before remembering you were hungry was to give us your stunning smile and you continued to smile throughout each day. That fantastic smile is now imprinted on many hearts and we long to see it again and to hear you giggle at the words 'keek', 'ping' and even just at the anticipation of being tickled.

You were never much of a sleeper, but really this meant we got to spend more time with you so we'll let you off. We rarely went longer than 2 or 3 hours without seeing your eyes wide open. And what beautiful, sparkly brown eyes they were! We treasured each and every cuddle with you and loved you snuggling into our left shoulders so much that IF you ever decided to nap during the day we would never lay you down.

We were so sad to see you having to go through chemo but you helped us lots by smiling your way through it all and by breaking all the rules. As your consultant once said as you continued to thrive throughout your treatment – 'Yes, but this is Oliver, he does things his own way'. Nothing bothered you – not even only having the full use of one arm – it was never an issue for you – you just made sure your other arm made up for it – constantly on the go and so fast too – so much that we were afraid you'd cause yourself an injury if your left arm started working at the same rate!

Everyone on the ward loved you, and they were miffed that we were so stingy in allowing others Oliver cuddles. You were called 'Gorgeous Boy' so often that we thought when you got to school and were asked what your name was, you would reply 'Gorgeous Boy Gill'.

We loved the times we had you at home, and tried to do as much as possible with you and no matter what it was, you loved it. You just loved life, and we ache that we are not going to see you grow up and do the many things we looked forward to seeing you do, and to doing with you. In a way, although tainted with fear of what might happen, your last 5 weeks at home with us were the best because we were a family at home together as it should always have been.

Although we knew you might not get better, we always believed you would. For reasons we may never understand, but try to trust in, you are now in an even happier place where finally Someone has been able to make you better. We would have done absolutely anything for you but that is something neither we, nor anyone else down here could do for you. Now though, you're in a place with no more central line or chemo, no more worry about cell counts, no more yucky medicines, no more attempts to make you eat baby rice and no need to wait any time at all for milk!

Not many babies can say they have over 2400 Facebook friends all over the world, and countless more not on Facebook. People loved getting to know you through your updates, photos and videos and we enjoyed the chance to show them what an amazing little guy you are. Everyone saw your beautiful eyes and smile, your cheeky face, trendy fashion sense, strong and loving friendships with Mr Monkey and Amos and how nothing stopped you from living your little life to the full.

Cancer is a hideous, ugly thing which you did not deserve and from which we are thankful you are now free. We know now that this was always going to be the outcome but we don't see why. We know good has and will come from your little but huge life story.

We are thankful for every second we were blessed with you. It is an honour and privilege to be your parents and to have been given such a beautiful, happy, brave and special baby to love and look after. No amount of time with you would ever have been enough, so five and a half months was definitely not. We know we will see you again one day and then we can play and cuddle forever without a care from this world. How wonderful it will be.

Oliver, we know you're safe, but we love and miss you desperately and more than we would ever have thought was possible. Your smile and your story will live on in many hearts and minds for a long time and not a second will ever go by when we don't think of, love, miss and long to see our gorgeous, gorgeous boy. We believe there is a reason for everything and we know your life came with many reasons. You changed our world forever and we just wish you were still here in it with us, even though we know for your sake it's better that you're not.

You've given us so many happy memories that we will treasure forever and you have taught us so much that no one would expect was possible for a baby.

You've shown us that medicine, science and humans don't have all the answers. You've taught us to make each day count and how to smile when our hearts are breaking. You literally turned night into day and made us grateful for everything. You've shown us the meaning of unconditional love and how to fully rely on God and praise Him in the storm. Your life was full of mini miracles and although we didn't get the big one we so longed for, we know that on that day, when we do get to hold you again, the reasons will be revealed and we will be humbled by them.

Oliver, you are so gorgeous and so amazing. We give you all our love and cuddles forever.

Love Mummy and Daddy

xxxxxxxxxxxxxxxxxx

Overcoming Evil

DISTRAUGHT, HEARTBROKEN, DEVASTATED. We found out what these words really mean as we stood at the graveside on New Year's Eve as Oliver's tiny casket was lowered into the ground. We had put our all into loving Oliver and caring for him, and over the last few weeks we had been constantly praying for and believing in a miracle, right up to the end. It felt so wrong and so surreal to be standing at the graveside. We were bereft of words, of prayers, of our hope for a cure and at a complete loss to make sense of it all.

Cancer is evil. The tumour had started changing shape because it was looking for ways to spread. Disgusting. Oliver was looking pale on the last couple of days because the tumour was stealing blood from the rest of his body. This evil, aggressive tumour was taking over our baby's otherwise perfect little body. It managed to defy and become resistant to intensive chemotherapy. It managed to grow and spread unnoticed, and by the time it did make itself known it was too late. The tumour was growing so much that the medics were prepared for the eventuality of the tumour breaking through the skin. If it had done so, the tumour would not have stopped bleeding. Oliver was spared from this just in time as this was very close to happening. Perhaps worst of all, the tumour managed to form in an innocent, helpless baby before he was even born. The cause and origin of this will never be known.

Cancer stole our baby. We always believed God would be with us on this journey, would make Oliver better and that Oliver would still be with us at the end of it. Even when the chemotherapy failed and there was no hope of surgery, we believed God would use a miracle to heal Oliver. We still believe He could have healed him but for some reason He chose not to. We know that this reason is good although we cannot understand it.

Cancer ruined our first family Christmas. As we look back on Christmas morning in our house the scene is so painful. Called by the nurse who had been with us all night, the doctor came through our living room door at seven in the morning to find us cuddling Oliver close to us on the couch, never wanting to let him go. Presents remained wrapped under the tree. We had been looking forward so much to our first Christmas with Oliver. We looked forward to coming down the stairs in the morning, opening presents together and playing with toys. Oliver would have loved everything about it.

There are not enough negative adjectives to describe cancer. We never thought we would be told there was no cure for Oliver. The day we were told there was no cure we were expecting plans for surgery. It had also come as a huge shock to the consultants. We sat down with Oliver's consultant and he told us the tumour was a lot bigger than they had thought – somehow it had managed to grow. We thought he would follow that with saying surgery would be further delayed. He then told us that the cancer had spread to Oliver's lungs. We thought he would then tell us treatment would be even longer. We never expected what came next, that in fact, there was no longer any hope of a cure for Oliver. We were left to go home to try to make the most of every moment with Oliver while at the same time watching the tumour grow, spread and take over our beautiful baby boy.

Cancer did not manage to stop us enjoying every minute we were blessed with Oliver. It did not manage to stop us cherishing him. It did not manage to stop him bringing so much joy in so many ways. It did not stop Oliver enjoying his little life to the full and making the most of each day. The mobility in Oliver's left arm was always affected to some degree. It now seems foolish that we were so upset that he may lose his arm. Losing his arm was an awful thought but we knew that it was better to have Oliver with a disabled arm or even no arm than not to have Oliver at all. If you did not look at Oliver's arm you would never have been able to tell there was anything wrong with him, and even looking at it you knew it was never going to be a problem for him. It was lovely seeing him use it when he could but it was never really an issue. Somehow, no matter how big the tumour got, it never seemed to bother him or cause him discomfort. He just got on with enjoying his toys, music, walks, cuddles, tickles, and of course his milk!

Cancer is evil. You need an attitude like Oliver's to be able to overcome its evil and that is why we would encourage everyone to support LoveOliver and other charities for children with cancer. Every day in the U.K. ten families are told their child has cancer. It kills more children than any other illness. We were oblivious to this before we had Oliver. To be told that a child only has weeks or months to live is unthinkable. It has been comforting for us to remember that other families have had similar experiences. It has been helpful to be in touch with them, even though this is the last thing anyone would want to have in common. LoveOliver is the charity we have set up for Oliver to help fund research into rare and aggressive cancers like the rhabdoid tumour Oliver had, and to provide practical help to families affected by childhood cancer. We want everyone to continue to Love Oliver and remember all that has come to us with Love from Oliver by supporting his cause.

Mini Miracles

IT IS STILL hard to believe that all this actually happened and ultimately ended so quickly. Before Oliver arrived, we always thought stories of childhood illness and death were awful but now we know what it is really like to love and lose your own child.

Oliver has changed our perspective on so many things and has shown us what is important in life. It was hard to see people carrying on as normal, enjoying Christmas and New Year, and returning to work when our lives will never be 'normal' again. We often have to bite our tongues when we hear people complaining about colds, teething, sleepless nights, vaccination jabs and all sorts of other things. How we would love to have to worry about these things! Before Oliver was born, these are things we would have complained about too, but now we know differently and know that anything else will pass or can be fixed. We have always been of the mind that you have to stay positive and make the most of everything, and we believe that even more now. We were able to love every minute with Oliver and be left with no regrets, because we just got on with enjoying him, and made the most of the situation in which we had found ourselves.

We wrote in our letter to Oliver that while we did not get the big miracle we so longed for, there were many mini miracles along the way. We feel it is important to point these out because they are so significant. We once heard a saying that 'In life there are no coincidences, just God incidents' and we really believe this is true.

Oliver weighed 9lbs 2oz when he was born – bigger than anyone would have expected from two petite people like us but also a good size to be ready to cope with all that was ahead of him. Oliver coped better with treatment than anyone expected. We have been told so often that a baby on chemotherapy should not have been feeding so well, and developing and growing so normally, while at the same time being so alert, chilled out and happy. We clearly remember one of the consultants talking to Oliver, amazed with his progress, saying, 'Chemo's easy, isn't it Oliver? Chemo's easy'. The nurses and doctors were also always amazed at the volumes of milk Oliver managed to guzzle down and the speed at which he managed it! He may have been the smallest person on the ward, but he had the biggest appetite.

Oliver was exclusively breastfed. This was a mixture of actual breastfeeding and expressed breast milk and we were told early on that the expressing, combined with the stress of the situation, would stop the breast milk early on. On the contrary, it continued and met his two to three hourly feed needs. Breast milk was best for Oliver and so that is what he got throughout.

We were always afraid Oliver would need to be tube fed and we were told this would more than likely happen. However, Oliver loved his food and fed so well that it was never necessary. This is very rare for a child on chemotherapy, especially a baby. There were two nurses carrying out a nutrition survey who said Oliver was going to wreck their statistics, as he continued to break all the rules throughout his treatment! His consultant said he had never seen anyone thrive or eat so much while on such intensive treatment. Oliver was always a perfect weight and size at each stage. Having made our baby sound like a thriving piglet we will now move on to the other mini miracles!

Oliver did not have a chance to have a routine. During his five and a half months we slept at Ninewells, on Wards 2 and 4 at Sick Kids, in numerous rooms at the CLIC house, at home, at Granny and Grandpa Black's, at Honorary Auntie Catriona's and at Great

Aunt Maggie's. Oliver was never able to have a routine but was so content all the time. He was not a cry baby apart from when deciding he was hungry. We were all often woken up during the night with nurses coming in and out when we slept on the ward, and during the day there was no time to sleep because of all the doctors, nurses, physiotherapists and visitors in and out of his room. One nurse joked that we needed a butcher's shop style ticket system for the number of people wanting to see Oliver. The lack of routine never bothered him. He just continued to relish all the attention and to fit in a few quick naps now and again.

We have both always been very susceptible to colds. Between July and the end of December we had none. If we had been ill and Oliver's counts were low we would have had to stay away from him. We are so thankful we stayed well.

Granny Black's retirement coming at the perfect time is another mini miracle. We could not have managed without her, and our photo albums of Oliver and Oliver's wardrobe and toy boxes would have been a lot less full without her input.

When we were finally sent home in November we were blessed with an amazing medical team. It is with great thanks to their dedication and care that we were able to keep Oliver at home right up until the morning of his funeral service. Oliver was assigned a consultant nearby in case we needed someone quickly. We already knew him through our minister/friend Neil. When he came to meet and assess Oliver he spoke from both his professional and Christian points of view, and he prayed for Oliver before leaving. The two community nurses assigned to us were people we already knew of through church. Their care for Oliver and for us was amazing. Off duty and taking time away from their own families, they spent most of December 22nd, 23rd and 24th in our house and arrived early on Christmas morning. After Oliver had passed away they bathed, dressed him and put him in his cot. They laid photos out and surrounded him with his toys. One would visit his room each day and even paid attention to things like making sure the lamp in his room was always on, and that his music was always playing. Whenever they or one of us went into his room it was almost as though the CD would just jump to the same track to play

> *'Safe in the Father's hands, you are safe in the Father's hands. 'Though there may be things you don't understand, you're safe in the Father's hands'.*[1]

The Forth Road Bridge was always the limit as far as Oliver's consultant was concerned when counts were low. We were almost tempted to drive across it just to see if he had set up an alarm system! Being at home was always important for us and another mini miracle is that once we came home in November we stayed at home, never crossing it again with Oliver. We took him to Deep Sea World – right next to the bridge on the Fife side and were proud not to cross it! There was always the possibility that Oliver might need to go to hospital, or to Rachel House but we were always determined to keep him at home. A doctor from Rachel House came to visit us on Christmas Eve. We were relieved when he said that from what he could see Oliver wasn't going to receive better care anywhere else but at home. From Christmas Day onwards we were also allowed to keep Oliver at home. His room needed to be cold enough for this to be possible and so at last we had a reason to be thankful for our cold, snowy winter. Having Oliver at home also helped us cope better with the funeral. Although our baby's perfect little body looked like a perfect little doll, lying in his cot in his room which he loved, Oliver had gone to Heaven where he would be safe and blissfully happy waiting for us to join him there. The Bible talks of our temporary earthly bodies as 'tents' and our eternal heavenly bodies as 'houses'. How stunning, gorgeous, amazing and perfect Oliver's house must be if this was his tent!

---

[1] Words by Paul Field © Meadowgreen Music Co/EMI Christian Music Publishing.

When Oliver was sent home in November there was meant to be a meeting between the Edinburgh and Fife medical teams to 'hand over' his case. This meeting was cancelled several times due to snowy weather. It finally took place on Wednesday 22nd December, the day Oliver was becoming very ill. While we were previously frustrated that the meeting had not yet taken place, we were so relieved and thankful that Oliver's consultant Mark was already on his way, on the day that we needed him most. Oliver was continuing to get the best medical care possible.

Oliver was never in pain or discomfort for long. On the last couple of days when he was in pain it would only be momentary because of the efficient way his nurses administered the pain relief. Once the cancer had spread to Oliver's brain the end was very quick. This too is a mini miracle. It could have gone on for days or weeks. The tumour could have broken through the skin under his arm, and also Oliver could have suffered fits. On Christmas morning when Oliver went to Heaven, knowing this was the way it was going to be, we found it almost a relief that his suffering was over. It was so peaceful.

Oliver's story has brought people of all ages together in prayer from all over the world. His story has touched so many lives and we have received hundreds of e-mails and cards from people whom we have never met. We have also had messages from people saying that they are grieving more deeply than they have ever done before, for this baby whom they never met, but felt they knew, and grew to love through his blog.

There are so many 'mini miracles' in Oliver's story and it is so obvious to us that God was at work from the start. All of them helped Oliver and ourselves to cope with what was being thrown at us, and all of them helped him to have the happiest little life possible, and to have a huge impact on so many people. The stunning smile which he developed from two weeks old also helped him to make a lasting impression. All the significant dates involved in his story only further confirm it was not all random coincidence. We don't understand the meaning. As in a film, when someone is about to crack a code, or solve a mystery that has been puzzling them for a long time – all the pieces of the jigsaw are coming together – and fit together perfectly – but the final piece, which reveals the answer, is still missing.

Praise Him in the Storm

SAYING WE DID not want to share our story is not entirely accurate. Of course we did not want it to be like this but we always planned to publish Oliver's Blog when he got better as a testimony to the greatness of God, the power of prayer and the amazing miracle which He'd performed in our lives by healing our baby. We never thought that our loving, powerful and faithful God would have planned Oliver's story to happen like this. But He did. And Oliver's Blog is still a testimony to the greatness of God, the power of prayer and the many 'mini miracles' which He performed in our lives through our baby.

Oliver's story has caused us to wrestle with and question God and His plan for us more than ever, but it has also made us hold on to His promises more tightly than ever before. We are often asked where our strength has come from – to plan Oliver's funeral ourselves, write our letter to him, set up his charity and website. The answer is simple – We can do all things through Christ who gives us strength (Phil. 4:13).

When praying for Oliver in the days leading up to Christmas we experienced a peace that we had never felt – the peace that passes all understanding that God promises to give us when we fully rely on Him (Phil. 4:5–8). We never understood how a peace so strong could possibly have been found in the fiery furnace or the lions' den. The peace we experienced as we faced our own fiery furnace certainly does pass understanding and explanation, but is most definitely real. Oliver's story has also caused us to really start living in the light of eternity, as the Bible tells us to do anyway. No matter how many questions we still have, we do ultimately know that the God who so clearly upheld us through Oliver's five and a half months, is the same God who is upholding us now. We've felt angry and disappointed with God but at the same time know that somehow this is all for a good purpose.

'He's in a happier place', 'He's been called Home', 'He's safe in God's hands' and 'He's now healed' are all nice thoughts but at the same time we think 'He was happy here', 'This was his home', 'He was safe in our hands', 'God could have healed him here'. No matter how much we try to focus on what he has been saved from, it still doesn't take away from the fact that he could have been healed or could have been well from the outset.

We don't ask 'Why Oliver?' because 'Why any baby?' We do ask 'Why?'. Why did God give us such an amazing gift only to take it away?. Why didn't God answer the thousands of prayers of thousands of people in the way everyone longed for? Why did God allow Oliver to have cancer in the first place? Why did God not step in and heal him? Why? Why? Why?

We don't have all the answers. We do know though that we could not have lived through Oliver's story in our own strength. We do know that everything happens for a reason. We know God works all things for good. We know God loves good and hates evil. We know enough about God from previous experiences in our lives and through what we read in the Bible that He can be trusted. We know we cannot understand everything and we know we have to trust God, even in the fiercest of storms. We're not called to say, 'Blessed be Your name *for* the road marked with suffering', rather we are called to say, 'Blessed be Your name *on* the road marked with suffering'. Praise You in the storm, not for the storm. God did not create Oliver's cancer or our suffering. However, He has used it and will use it in ways we cannot understand but can trust are good. We do not thank God for the illness or for our suffering but we do thank Him for the good He has brought and will continue to bring from it. Life is full of disappointments, some far more sore than others. God promises that those who put their trust in Him will not be disappointed and we fully believe that.

This could be seen as a very cruel story, culminating in the events of Christmas Day being the saddest day of our lives. We were given a lot of hope throughout Oliver's life which made us believe he would get better. This hope came to us through the medics being so positive, Oliver coping so well and amazing everyone, things people would say to us, verses we read from the Bible, songs we listened to and from the great sense of peace we had about the whole situation. We know we needed hope beyond hope to keep us positive for Oliver – for him to be happy, for us to enjoy him and to be able to give him the care he needed.

We blogged on Christmas Eve about a Bible reading we had done together with Oliver which really made us believe that he would be healed. We let some friends know about it and asked them to pray and some of them say they had felt like they never had done before, and were confident that something amazing was about to happen. We don't know why we were given this hope on Christmas Eve. It has been suggested that Oliver was healed the very next morning, so that hope was followed through, just not in the way we so longed for. As far as hoping that Oliver's rainbow would come soon, we know that in the Christian life, the ultimate rainbow, the peace after the storm, is heaven, and therefore Oliver has received His full blessings.

We wrote in the blog that, while we couldn't understand why Oliver wasn't healed instantly in our preferred timescale, that we trusted that God's timing is perfect. That remains true, God's timing is perfect. Oliver was fourteen days late for a reason, he was sent home from hospital in time to give us five precious weeks at home as a family, Mark his consultant was already on his way to our home on the day we needed him most, Oliver was taken from us before the tumour had a chance to break through the skin or before he experienced fits. Perhaps most significantly he was called to Heaven on Christmas Day, the day that is set aside to celebrate God sending His own Son to the world to live and die for us. When we were sent home from hospital we were told Oliver could pass away before Christmas or that he might live for several months longer. It is no coincidence that the dawn of Christmas Day was Oliver's time. A special day for a very special boy, as so many people have said to us. Now that we are able to look back on all the significant dates and mini miracles in Oliver's life, it almost makes sense that he went to Heaven on Christmas Day.

We always thought it made sense for Oliver to have a long life in which to glorify God. We thought that if man's chief aim is to glorify God then Oliver would need to grow up to serve Him. How wrong we were! In his very short life Oliver managed to glorify God more than any of us will manage in a lifetime, and he did this without ever saying a word! He has taught many people about God's love without ever reaching the stage of talking. He has shown us the power of God and how His ways are definitely not our ways, but His ways are the best. In twenty-four weeks Oliver touched more lives than many of us will do in a lifetime, and influenced them more deeply in the process. People across the world have wept for Oliver even though they never knew him or ourselves. Oliver's lifesong sings of God and to God. It brought and continues to bring smiles to thousands. He was chosen by God and was privileged to be used in ways bigger than we can grasp. Oliver was created by God to fulfil a big mission in a very short time. The mini miracles that even our human minds have been able to recognise are only scratching at the surface of a much bigger master plan.

Neither of us had really experienced major loss in our lives. We have both lost grandparents and as sad as that is, it is nothing compared to the pain of losing your own baby through a devastating illness. Our experience of death is not what many would expect. It is not dark, hopeless, unknown and scary. It is peaceful, it made sense in the circumstances, it is non-threatening and it is full of hope. We know we could not keep Oliver with us no matter how much we wanted to, and while the pain is still deep and real and always will be, we know that we will see Oliver again. We say we would do absolutely anything to have Oliver back, but we do not have to do anything because Jesus has done it for us by dying on the cross, to give us eternal life, together again. It will never take away the ache of wanting Oliver here now, but it does give us the hope of spending forever with him. Oliver is now enjoying the life he deserves, eternal life of total bliss and happiness. Oliver was oblivious to the pain and suffering involved in his life. All he knew was happiness, love, fun and cuddles and we will one day be able to enjoy all those things with him again, forever. Oliver will never know what it is like to experience pain, heartache, illness or death. We cannot know much about what heaven is like, for it is a matter of faith and is too great to even start to imagine. We do know though that Jesus is there and Oliver is there, and for us it does not need to get any better than that!

The Beginning

THE FACT THAT Oliver is now in Heaven makes the idea of Heaven even more wonderful to us. We long to see him again – to cuddle him, hear his giggles, play with him and never have to let him go. Not having Oliver here with us gets harder as it becomes more real and 'normal', because obviously we do not want it to be either. We know that life does go on, but we also know that it will now always include the pain and empty feeling of Oliver not being here physically with us. Nothing can or will heal this, not even time. Time does not heal – it merely forces you to find ways to cope and continue in life. The longing for Oliver is just as strong if not stronger each day – always picturing how different life would be if he was still with us, and imagining what he would be like at each different stage. The good thing about time is that it is moving us ever closer to him.

We always looked forward so much to being at home with Oliver. That has not changed, apart from knowing that next time we're at Home with him it will be forever. We know we are still here because God still has a purpose for us, and so life goes on for that purpose, and goes on thankfully with the sure hope we have of being reunited with our baby.

We like to think that Oliver is asleep in Heaven until we join him there. It is hard for us to think of him being with other people, when our strong parental instincts tell us we should be the ones looking after him and when we are constantly longing for him to be in our own arms. We know Oliver is in Heaven and is safe, and if he is asleep (although considering his efforts here we can't be too sure!) then it would mean he would have fallen asleep in his Mummy's arms, and would wake up in them, so he would not know anything different. This is a comforting thought for us, but we know that all that really matters is that we have the assurance that he is safe in the Father's arms and that we will see him again. Whatever happens, we know it's good although our human minds cannot comprehend it. We think within the limits of time, and are comforted by knowing that, to Oliver, there will seem to be no passage of time between him getting to Heaven and us joining him. However, we are presently going through a very long passage of time during which we will always miss him, love him and long to see him. Sometimes we almost feel detached from what is going on, because it feels as if it could not all have happened, and in such a short space of time. At other times it feels so real and painful it hurts.

Seeing baby clothes and toys in the shops, little kids out on their bikes or getting kiddy backs, hearing their laughs, cries and childlike voices, going into Oliver's little bedroom, and picturing how different life would be if he was still here are all so hard. We will learn to cope with being parted from our baby but the pain will never go away. Oliver will always be our first baby and will be the big brother to any other children we may have. He will always be talked about, remembered and longed for every day. Oliver's love of life and cheeky smile are captured forever in our hundreds of photos of him – in his busy five and a half months he made sure he would not be forgotten. We have many photos of Oliver on display in our house and have made sure that there is at least one in every room. His gorgeous smile is with us every day, and not many minutes go by without him being mentioned or without happy memories of him being shared.

Knowing now that this was always going to be the outcome, we would not change anything about it. No matter how painful and difficult the journey was, it was also one full of many joys and blessings. We know Oliver received the best medical care possible and from the best team of people possible. We know we did everything we could for him and we now know that nothing could have changed the outcome. One of us was always with him and we never left him to cry. He even got into our bed a few times which he loved. These may not have been the best parenting techniques but they were the best for Oliver and made him as happy as possible. Knowing Oliver was so happy through it all and did not suffer discomfort or pain is a real comfort and blessing. For that reason we can truly say that we would do it all again if it meant having and knowing Oliver, even for far too short a time. For want of a better expression, it is definitely better to have loved and lost than never to have loved at all, even though with all our hearts we wish he was still here with us.

Finding a way to conclude this book is difficult. The book may be at an end but Oliver's story will live on forever. Oliver showed us how imperfect this life really is and has given us a glimpse of eternity. This life can never fully satisfy us and this world is not our home. Through Oliver, God has changed our perspective on everything and while we know there will still be good things in this life, we now live in the light of the hope of a life far greater than this. C.S Lewis concludes the Chronicles of Narnia by saying:

> *'And for us this is the end of all the stories, and we can most truly say that they all lived happily ever after. But for them it was only the beginning of the real story. All their life in this world and all their adventures in Narnia had only been the cover and the title page: now at last they were beginning Chapter One of The Great Story which no one on earth has read: which goes on forever: in which every chapter is better than the one before.'*[1]

---

[1] The Last Battle © copyright C.S. Lewis Pte. Ltd 1956.

Oliver's Blog is only his cover page and title, and we long for the day when we get to start The Great Story with Oliver, back in our arms, together at last, together forever. How wonderful it will be.

Love for Oliver

OLIVER'S BLOG WAS updated regularly on Facebook and sent out weekly by e-mail. Right from the outset we were overwhelmed by the response it received, but most of all from 18th November onwards. It was on that day we were told a medical cure for Oliver was no longer possible. At that point the blog had 755 members. A week later the number had more than doubled and even after Christmas Day it continued to increase, reaching over 2400.

From 18th November, not an hour went by without messages of support being written to us. If we had published the whole of the blog with all comments included, this book would be an epic! The following are just some of the hundreds of messages that we received from Christmas Day onwards from around the world. We have put them together as a tribute to the short but inspirational life of our gorgeous baby Oliver ...

> '... Oliver has been such a blessing with his incredible strength and smile. He touched the lives of so many through this blog. xx'

> '... God is still working through Oliver's life to bring people close to Him. God does have a much bigger plan, and we pray that one day you will be shown this plan. He was such a bright little boy and he touched our hearts even without ever meeting him ...'

'... I also pray you take comfort and courage from the true blessing and inspiration Oliver was to your lives and the fact that your journey touched and inspired so many people and brought them close to God. Even in his passing, Oliver continues to touch so many people's hearts ...'

'... we uphold you in our prayers as you face the loss of your wonderful little boy. He has touched so many of our hearts and we pray now that God will give you the strength and support as you deal with your loss. Thank you for sharing Oliver with us − he has been the first thing in our minds as we awake every morning and the last thing before we go to sleep at night − thank you for coming into all our lives, Oliver.'

'Little Oliver, you lit up so many lives and touched so many people and will be greatly missed by all. It is comforting to know that you are now forever in God's house and in His arms ...'

'I am so sorry to hear about your loss. You have all been in my thoughts throughout today. There are not many little boys in this world who had over 2000 people worldwide who loved, cared and prayed for him. Each one of us checking in every day for the latest update on his blog. God bless you all.'

'You are all in our thoughts and prayers today. We can't even imagine your pain, but we know that God can give you all the strength and comfort you need. Oliver will never be forgotten, he has truly touched the lives of many, even those who didn't meet him. You guys are amazing. X'

'... What a precious gift he was and what a wonderful blessing he will continue to be ...'

'You and your beautiful baby have touched all our hearts over these past months, challenging and inspiring us and we feel a real sense of loss today too ... We were privileged to have been part of Oliver's life. Thank you both. xxx'

'Oliver: a small person with a very short life who accomplished a tremendous amount. He brought people together in prayer around the world. He reminded us that science doesn't have all the answers, and that the Lord moves in mysterious ways.'

'I know there is nothing we can say apart from how amazing and gorgeous your boy was.'

'We weep with you but we are so grateful for the ministry of Oliver's Blog, and the impact the three of you have had in so many lives across the world, to God's glory.'

'You will be in the hearts of those that you have touched forever, the strength of your parents is inspirational and you will live on in them everyday. I know that their incredible faith will be what carries them through and the loving support they have will help them heal. We will miss you terribly but we won't forget. xx'

'We grieve all over the world for a beautiful smiling boy who touched the hearts of thousands of people. You too Jennifer and Andy – your faith has been such a witness to us all and you have touched our hearts too. We thank you for sharing your journey with Oliver with us and we continually pray for you both as you now face life without him. We cannot understand why, only trust our loving God as He knows best.'

'At times like this words don't seem adequate at capturing the feelings but I want to say thank you. Thank you for having such a beautiful boy who has melted our hearts, thank you for allowing us all to share your journey, thank you for being such a strong and gracious witness and thank you to God who is holding Oliver dear to him. I pray that God will be with you all and carry some of your pain. Sent with tears of love. xx'

'... Your willingness to allow us into your private lives has been testimony to your wonderful faith. Your wee darling has given us joy in seeing his photos, tears as we have wept over his situation, and yours, but mostly thankfulness that he was given to two such wonderful parents for his all too short time on this earth. God will honour your faith ...'

'... I know in Oliver's short life he has been used as a massive testimony to many. Lives have been changed because of your little boy ...'

'... God's purpose for us ultimately is that we will glorify Him, and Oliver has done that so beautifully. He has lifted our eyes to Him ...'

'... Our hearts ache for you in the loss of your precious little boy. Little Oliver has touched so many folk, and your shining faith has humbled us and strengthened our own ...'

'It's a fantastic way we have all been brought together to pray for Oliver and his family. I don't think I have ever prayed so hard or so much in my life.'

'We are all part of God's big family and we hurt when we know our fellow Christians are hurting. I have never prayed so much either, what a wonderful little baby, what a wonderful family, what a wonderful God. xx'

'... No child could be loved more than wee Oliver. No child ever drew so many people closer to the Lord. Oliver's name will forever be linked to the happy, trusting thoughts Jen and Andy shared on the blog on his behalf ...'

'Your gorgeous boy has had such a massive effect on everyone and his smile has brought thousands of people together. Your pictures and letter were stunning and showed Oliver to be such a happy, loving boy. It's a small but reassuring thought that he is being looked after, and he is smiling on Gods left shoulder until he sees his mummy and daddy again. Your son has already played a huge part in making this world a better place. All my love and thoughts are with you. xx'

'What a sweet testimony precious Oliver's story has been. By God's grace his little life has been such an inspiration to so many people in this fallen world where there is so much need for hope and joy!! In God's grace He has used this to make life and joy triumph over death and sadness. May He be with you both in a mighty way and continue to use you for His glory.'

'May I make a suggestion? Perhaps one day you could write Oliver's story. Many families have and sadly will find themselves in your position. Oliver's story and how you coped, decisions you faced, dealing with the highs and unfathomable lows, all would be a

wonderful help. My extended family have lost several
little ones over the years and the pain is still felt.
Having something like the Gill story would have been
a wonderful blessing. May God bless you even more
richly and thank you for sharing this child of Christ. In
the photo of your three hands, there is another, unseen
and pierced, may you always know His strength and
comfort.'

Wow. How incredible that all of these thoughts were shared about
our five and a half month old baby! Oliver certainly was given to us
to fulfil a big purpose in a short time.

Continuing to Love Oliver

AS PREVIOUSLY MENTIONED, LoveOliver is the charity we have set up in memory of our darling Oliver. We chose the name because it has the double meaning of continuing to Love Oliver and remembering all that he brought to us, with Love from Oliver. As you will see in the logo – Oliver's name includes the letters of 'love' which makes Love Oliver an even more fitting name for his charity.

Having been on such a journey with Oliver we could not simply carry on without trying to make a difference to others who face a similar journey. Our aim for LoveOliver is to help to fund research into childhood cancer as well as to provide practical help to families affected by it.

LoveOliver was set up as a trust fund in January 2011 and became a fully registered charity in July 2011. By April over £19,000 had already been raised for the fund, and at the time of this book going to print, over £40, 000 has been raised through generous donations and fundraising events.

We are greatly encouraged by the number of people signing up for different sponsored events, and organising fundraising activities in aid of LoveOliver. These have included coffee mornings, sponsored events such as cycling, running, walking, zumba, swimming, curry nights, concerts, auctions, non-uniform days, and even spacehopping across the Forth Road Bridge! Even people we have never met are getting involved because of the impact Oliver's story has had on them.

It is a privilege to have already donated £20, 000 to a research project into the rare and aggressive type of cancer which Oliver had.

The LoveOliver website was launched on 27th January and has already had visits from nearly sixty different countries. We really hope LoveOliver will be around for a long time to come. Please support the charity in any way you can – pray, donate, fundraise, get involved. You can find out all you need to know and see photos from all the events at www.loveoliver.org.uk.

So Many Thank Yous ...

WE HAVE SO many people we would like to thank for the many things they have done for Oliver and ourselves ...

Oliver's consultant Mark Brougham. On our first day at the hospital all the staff were so kind to us that we thought there must be some 'niceness test' that they had to pass to work there. Then we met Mark and remember commenting to each other that he must have passed that test with flying colours! Mark has been a huge support to us from the start.

All the amazing staff on Ward 2 at The Royal Hospital for Sick Children in Edinburgh and at the CLIC house for their genuine care.

Michelle Aitken and Gill Deaves from Children's Community Nurses - Fife, Tricia Johnstone and Pat Carracher from CHAS, Oliver's health visitor Fiona Kemp, and Dr John Morrice who all went above and beyond the call of duty for Oliver and for ourselves. We will never forget their kindness.

Our friend Rev Neil MacMillan for all the time he spent with us, for praying with us and for us, for his shoulder to cry on, for leading the service to celebrate Oliver's life and for continuing to support us.

Kirkcaldy Free Church and Buccleuch Free Church for providing meals for us to make life a lot easier.

Newcraigs Church, Rev Kevan Leckie and Sheila Matthew for helping so much with the preparations for Oliver's funeral service and with practical support on the day.

Oliver's Uncle Alasdair Black for encouraging us to start Love-Oliver and for all his hard work in the charity registration process and in his role as treasurer. Thank you too to Douglas Aitken, Kate Murray and Linda Scott for agreeing to be trustees and for all their support.

Our wonderful parents, families and friends who were there for us in many, many ways during the ups and downs of Oliver's twenty four weeks, and who have continued to be a massive support to us.

All those keeping up to date with Oliver's Blog on Facebook and e-mail – those we know and those we don't know, who have so faithfully supported us in prayer, and who have sent us hundreds of messages of encouragement and support. Thank you for buying this book and for reading Oliver's story.

And above all, thank you to God – for blessing us with Oliver, for twenty-four weeks of treasured memories, for providing for us and for being with us, for strength to keep going, for whatever His reasons in all of this may be, because we know they are good, and for the hope we have of Heaven and of being reunited with our Gorgeous Boy.

> '*So we fix our eyes not on what is seen, but on what is unseen. For what is seen is temporary, but what is unseen is eternal*' (2 Cor. 4:18 *NIV*)

Thank you all,

Love Andy and Jennifer

Oliver's 1st Birthday – July 10th – A Very Special Day

OUR EXPERIENCE WITH Oliver has changed our perspective on everything and has put everything into perspective. One of these things is the significance of special days and celebrations as they are so different for us now. They would be hard anyway but with Oliver choosing to make his mark on all of them, they are even more poignant for us now and don't have the importance that they once had. It would seem wrong however, not to mention on Oliver's Blog, a very special day coming up this weekend.

In a few days time it will be Oliver's 1st birthday – not just another 'monthirthday' but his actual 1st birthday. How it is even possible that he would be one already we do not know! How we long to know one year old Oliver and how we long for every little thing about him every single day.

While we long for balloons, cards, presents, his little friends round to his house and his little cheeky face covered in cake, giggling his way through July 10th, we are trying to keep remembering that our baby boy was created for a much bigger purpose than we can ever understand.

July 10th is a very special day. It is the day that Oliver Gill came into our lives and changed them in more ways than we could ever have expected. It is a day when we can thank God for our beautiful baby, and for His purpose in bringing him into our lives and making this little guy the biggest part of our family. It is a day when we can question and wrestle with how different the pages God wrote for

Oliver look to the ones that we would have written. It is a day when we can't even begin to imagine how wonderful the celebration will be and how special the day will be when Oliver is back in our arms forever, and it is a day that we can remember what a blessing and a privilege it is to be Oliver's parents.

Of course these thoughts and feelings apply to us every day and every day without Oliver here is so hard. However, Oliver's 1st birthday is special as it marks one year since those stunning sparkling eyes and that beautiful smile came into our lives. It was a day full of emotion, excitement and expectation. We miss him more than we would ever be able to put into words and we are thankful for everything about him and for the blessing that he continues to be, and will always be. July 10th is Oliver's very own special day. Happy first birthday to our Gorgeous Boy.

Love Mummy and Daddy xxxxxxxxxxxx

Christian Focus Publications

publishes books for all ages

STAYING FAITHFUL

In dependence upon God we seek to impact the world through literature faithful to His infallible Word, the Bible. Our aim is to ensure that the Lord Jesus Christ is presented as the only hope to obtain forgiveness of sin, live a useful life and look forward to heaven with Him.

REACHING OUT

Christ's last command requires us to reach out to our world with His gospel. We seek to help fulfill that by publishing books that point people towards Jesus and help them develop a Christ-like maturity. We aim to equip all levels of readers for life, work, ministry and mission.

Books in our adult range are published in three imprints.

CHRISTIAN FOCUS contains popular works including biographies, commentaries, basic doctrine and Christian living. Our children's books are also published in this imprint.

MENTOR focuses on books written at a level suitable for Bible College and seminary students, pastors, and other serious readers. The imprint includes commentaries, doctrinal studies, examination of current issues and church history.

CHRISTIAN HERITAGE contains classic writings from the past.

Christian Focus Publications, Ltd
Geanies House, Fearn, Ross-shire,
IV20 1TW, Scotland, United Kingdom
info@christianfocus.com
www.christianfocus.com